Abi Kremer

Colour and Inspiration

Paintings 1979 - 2009

Jackie Sarafopoulos

Foreword: Professor Simon Olding

Introductory Essay: Peter Davies

Modern Times Art Publications

Abi Kremer

Colour and Inspiration

Paintings 1979 - 2009

Published by Modern Times Art Publications

Bournemouth

moderntimes@live.co.uk

1st published December 2009

Designed by Summerhouse

ISBN 978-0-9564418-0-5

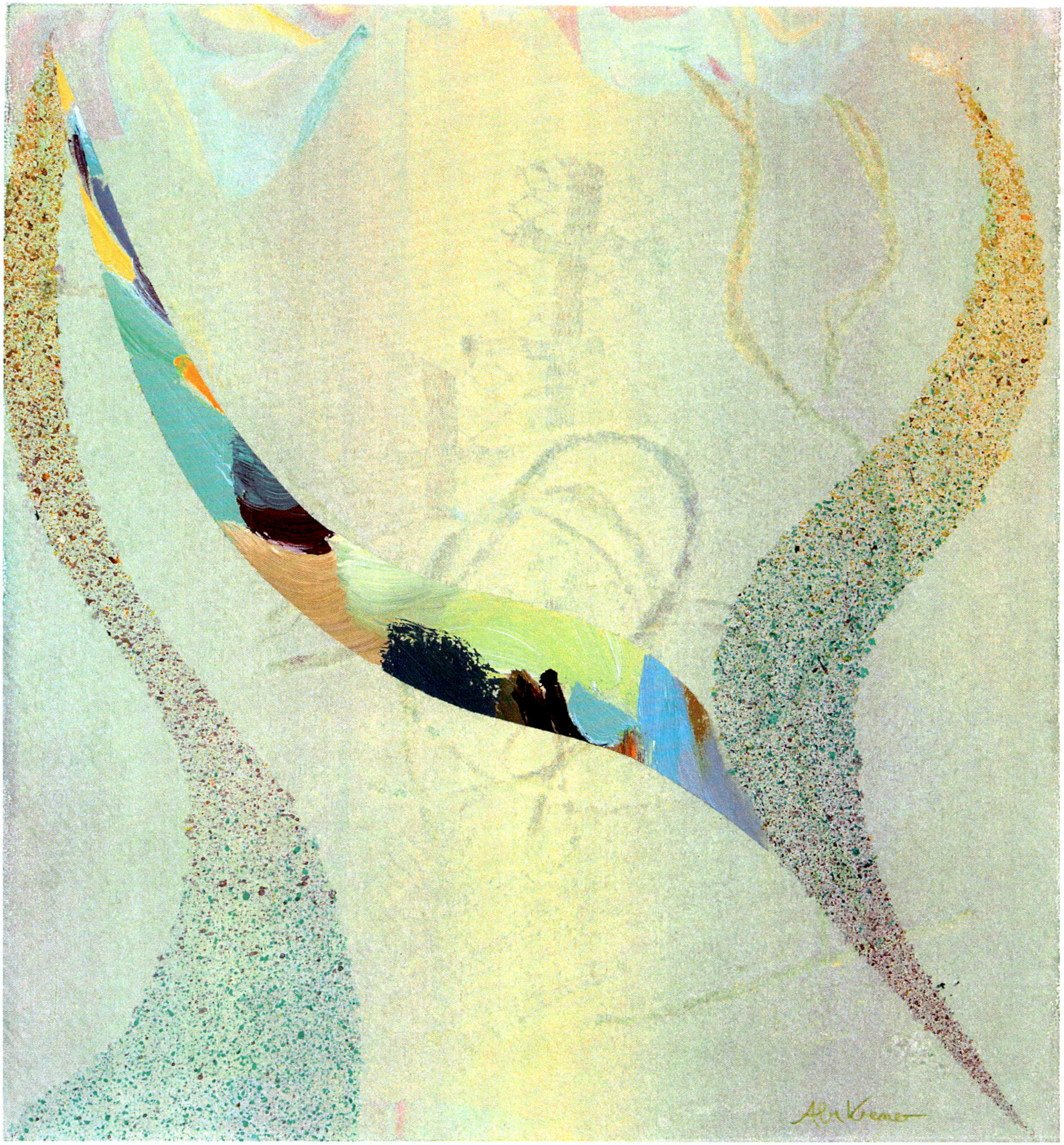

Kami Print Series 4 2007
Mono screenprint
25cm x 20cm

Abi Kremer

Foreword

Abi Kremer's touch as an artist is light, sometimes fugitive. The evocative mood that she seeks to establish in her paintings and prints is often one with a meditative character. Yet if the touch is light, then it is also brisk or calligraphic. In her latest paintings, structured elements appear against washed, dream-like backdrops. Luminous colour is presented as an energy field.

Abi's first substantive painting was the fine abstract *Reflection,* praised by Prunella Clough, and though a student work, impressively and elegantly structured. She used her technical skills in drawing to carry her adventure forward into a career as a professional artist, although she focused very quickly on abstraction. The influences on her work also multiplied, enabling her to find more complex ways of developing images which combined, equally, the physical reality of a place (sea or river, woodland or a more imagined landscape) with the mood and atmosphere inherent in it. These influences, from St Ives, Abstract Expressionism, Oriental calligraphy and Surrealism, have been melded into a distinctive personal style. A meditative energy is explicit in an Abi Kremer work, made manifest with a sensitive luminosity. Her art comes from a good heart and a generous humanity.

This humanity has also enabled Abi to forge long-standing and very productive relationships with many of the cultural institutions which are close to her Bournemouth home. Notable amongst these is the agreeably idiosyncratic Russell-Cotes Art Gallery and Museum, the setting in 2005 for one of the first solo exhibitions in a newly created prints and drawings room, and a venue for many of Abi's inspiring teaching sessions.

In more contemporary buildings (the Russell-Cotes is, at its heart, a Victorian Villa, albeit one on a grand scale) Abi has also made effective contributions. She was determined enough to secure her first solo exhibition at the Poole Arts Centre in 1987, and more recently she has been commissioned to create site-specific pieces for hospitals, including those in Salisbury and Bournemouth. These works build on her natural sympathies as a communicator and as a teacher.

Abi's creative work with these institutions reveals her innate ability as a planner of complex projects and as an innovative educator keen to stretch her students and unlock the potential of private places through art. She is a loyal friend to all of these organisations. Currently, her work takes place in a studio setting in the gentle landscape setting of Holton Lee, Poole, where the surrounding woodlands offer evocative imagery for her new inquiry into the natural world. It is a place of poise and inner harmony, just as Abi's work, at its best, is both gentle of spirit and finely considered. Her light touch is the touch of experience and the outcome of careful reflection. Her seemingly spontaneous mark-making is both deeply considered and humanely expressed.

Professor Simon Olding

Professor Simon Olding has had a varied career in the arts and museum sectors since 1979. His most recent senior posts have been Head of Arts and Museums for Bournemouth Borough Council (and Director of the acclaimed Russell-Cotes Art Gallery and Museum) and Director of Policy and Research, Heritage Lottery Fund. He joined the University for the Creative Arts as Director of the Crafts Study Centre in 2002 and was appointed Professor of Contemporary Crafts in 2003.

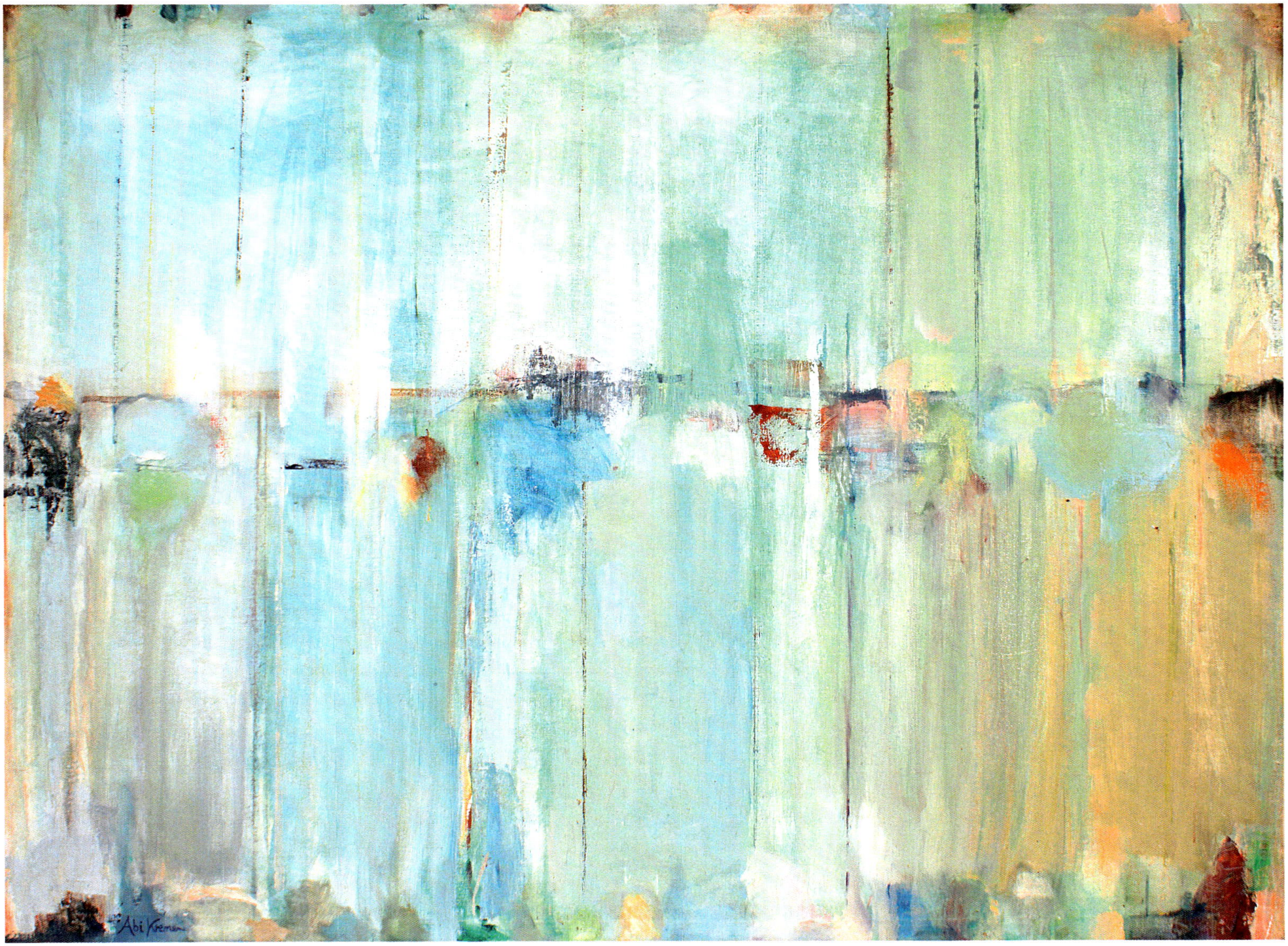

Reflections 1977
Oil on canvas
135cm x 180cm

Abi Kremer

In Context

The paintings of Abi Kremer celebrate growth, movement and light. They are executed with thin, dilute but vivid solutions of pale, pastel-like oil colour and possess the airy transparency and diaphanous subtlety of a watercolourist. While landscape is a source of inspiration and even indeed an oblique frame of reference, she does not generally approach landscape using the topographical references of the traditional watercolourist. Rather Kremer pursues a modernist vein of nature-inspired abstraction in which intuitive colour, gestural-mark making and a vital creative tension between surface and depth creates compelling analogies with nature.

While these unmistakably painterly analogies with nature set her work within the soft tranquil poetry and landscape romanticism of the 'English School', the overall stylistic complexion is broadly 'abstract expressionist', drawing on the gestural immediacy of 'New York School' painters like Franz Kline, Willem de Kooning, Morris Louis and Helen Frankenthaler. de Kooning's early identification with the figure notwithstanding, these four American painters often created deliberate or inadvertent pictorial equivalents of the landscape sublime. Bennington-trained Frankenthaler's early *'Mountains and Sea'* attained the atmospheric suggestiveness and awesome grandeur of the tradition of the American sublime and in so doing tempered the novelty of the 'New American Painting' with deference to older art historical currents.

In the contemporaneous British situation, one reflecting both longstanding transatlantic cultural links and status as a paid-up European country, native tradition decreed compromise between past and present and modifications of modernism. Within this context Kremer's informalism sits squarely with St. Ives 'middle generation' abstraction*1, with the metropolitan 'Metavisual, Taschiste, Abstract' group (Redfern Gallery London 1957)*2 who looked as much to lyrical or concretist 'Ecole de Paris' art as to New York, and to outstanding individuals like the Sussex-based Ivon Hitchens. Evident in the work of St. Ivesers' like Peter Lanyon, Bryan Wynter and Patrick Heron or of Hitchens, was not only reference to landscape as a repository both of history and of human or natural geography, but an allusion to 'spirit of place', or the unique 'genius loci', that haunting British identification with ancient locations.

Born in London in 1955 and educated at South Hampstead High School for Girls before studying first at Harrow (1973-74) then Bournemouth College of Art (1974-77), Kremer has spent almost her entire career in Bournemouth, establishing a local reputation alongside other leading contemporary Dorset artists like Martyn Brewster, Brian Graham, Padraig Macmiadhachain, Alastair Michie, Peter Joyce, Geoffrey Robinson, Stan Davis and Jeremy Gardiner. Collectively they have contributed to a perceived modern art movement in Dorset, one to supplement, if not displace, the unrivalled Cornish 'school'. Certainly during the thirty-plus years I have known her, Abi Kremer has contributed in no small measure to the blossoming south-east Dorset art scene.

*1 This St. Ives 'middle generation', a nickname supposedly coined by the London art dealer Leslie Waddington, were the abstracting landscape-derived painters who were based in post-war Cornwall. Following the senior figures of Ben Nicholson, Barbara Hepworth and Naum Gabo they included Peter Lanyon, Terry Frost, Patrick Heron and Bryan Wynter.

*2 The exhibition with a catalogue foreword by Denys Sutton was a broad ranging survey of contemporary British abstract art with an emphasis on painterly, automatic or process-based painting. Among the 34 exhibiting artists were Frank Avray Wilson, Gillian Ayres, Sanda Blow, Denis Bowen – who Kremer met in Swanage in 2004 – John Coplans, Alan Davie, Patrick Heron, Peter Lanyon, Ralph Rumney, Bryan Wynter and Alan Reynolds. Ayres's contribution 'Tachiste Painting 5' (1957) was a blaze of brightly coloured poured and thrown paint. Ayres, who Kremer met at Southampton City Art Gallery, produced a dinning room mural for the Hampstead school which Kremer attended during the 1960's and this large, powerful piece of public pictorial art made its presence felt on an impressionable, artistically inclined schoolgirl.

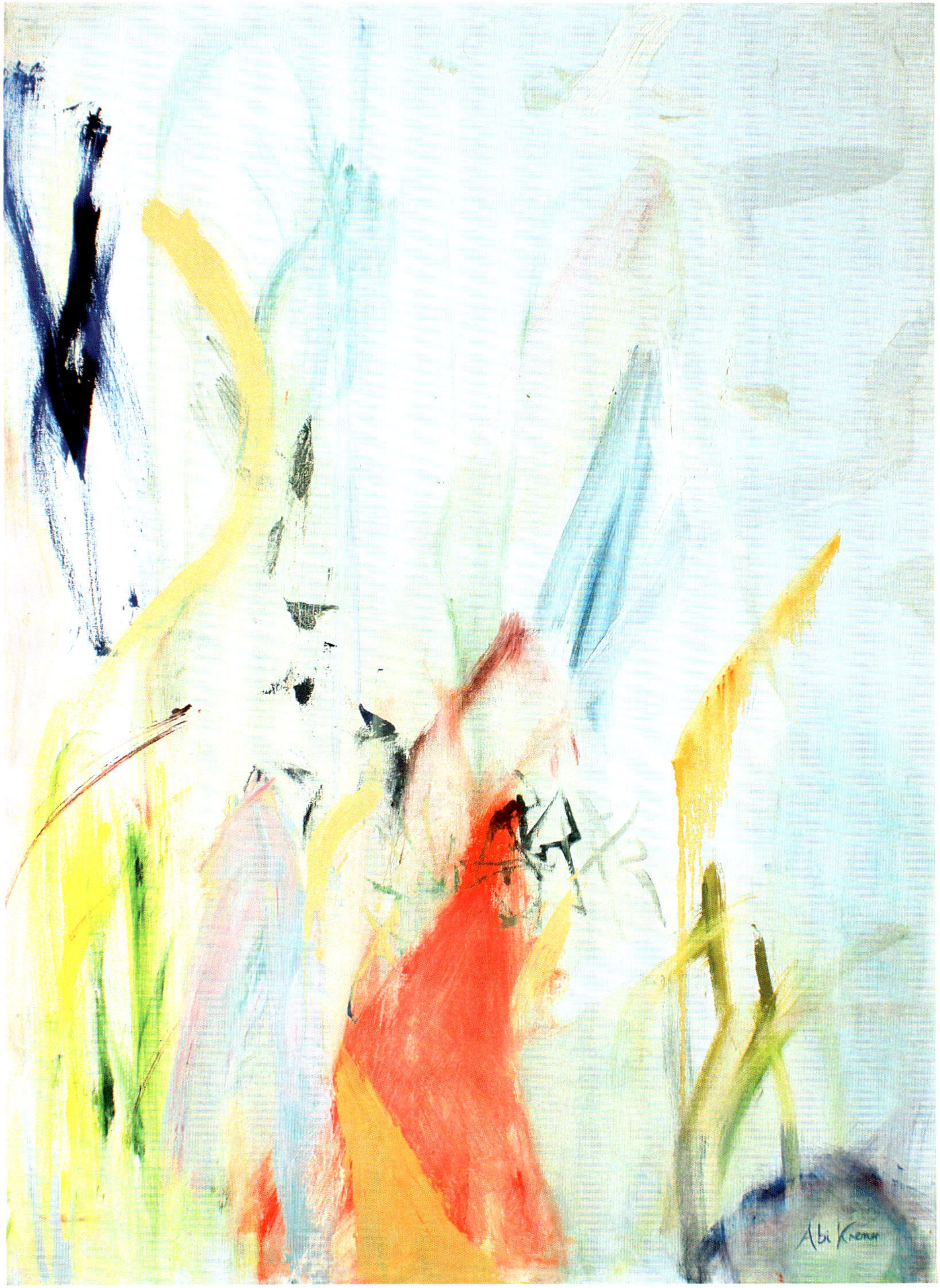

Garden 1 1981
Oil on canvas
150cm x 105cm

Abi Kremer

In Context

At the 'Modern Artists Exhibition' organised by Jack Lane and I at the Russell-Cotes Museum, Bournemouth in early 1979, Kremer showed the large canvas *'Reflections'* alongside work by Lanyon, Barbara Hepworth, John Hoyland, Frank Bowling, Anthony Caro and others, and from that time she has tempered the sobriety of a family-orientated suburban lifestyle in which picture-making has happily remained a constant, not-so-background activity with an ambition informed and inspired by admiration for those leading, historically significant artists, some of whom she has periodically, if fleetingly, met. In similar vein Kremer's coverage in 'Art in Poole and Dorset' (1987), my mainly historical study of inter and post war art in south-east Dorset, highlighted the progress of a still young painter who was putting on, or soon to put on, solo exhibitions at Seldown Gallery, Poole Arts Centre (1987), Old Town Hall Gallery, Havant (1989), The Gantry, Southampton (1990) and much later at Russell-Cotes (2005). During the last 20 years she has also made further progress through the medium of the group exhibition, displaying work further afield in 'My Generation' at Atkinson Gallery, Southport (1989), in 'Blue' at Beatrice Royal Art Gallery, Eastleigh (1995) and in 'A Postcard from St. Ives' (2007) at Belgrave Gallery, St. Ives.

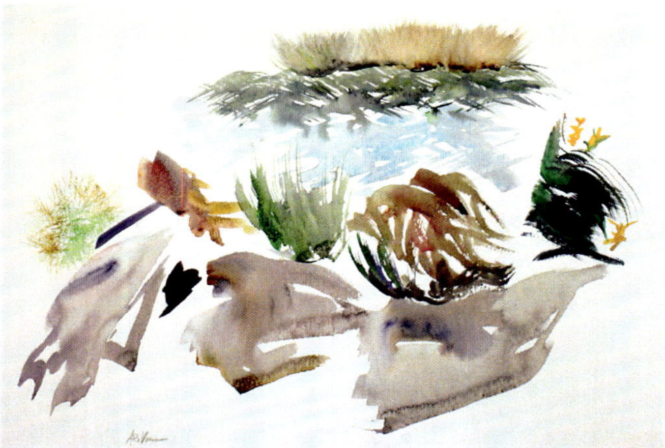

Hengistbury Head 2002
Watercolour
30cm x 50cm

The term expressionist may seem a misnomer for a painter of such refinement and delicate sensibility but the breadth and subtlety of her palette, looseness of handling accommodating chance and accident and embracing of space and scale positions her closer to expressionism than to descriptive naturalism. At Harrow Kremer did a project on German Expressionism; her 1977 thesis at Bournemouth, for which she gained a distinction, was on Japanese prints, a subject of prime art historical significance for any student of late 19th and early 20th century art (Gauguin, Van Gogh, Whistler and the Nabis were all influenced). Kremer's style is not conducive to the flat, mechanically-rendered forms of the Japanese woodcut. She has intermittently branched out into printmaking using the freer 'painterly' process of screen print in preference to the mechanical rigors of the relief print*3. But her contemplative natural vision and penchant for direct, unmediated paint handling borrows from Japanese and Chinese calligraphy, one of the most ancient manifestations of visual culture. If Picasso, Braque and Derain looked to the dark continent and to tribal carving in a quest to see form anew then other, perhaps less formal but more decorative painters adapted the quieter elegance of traditional oriental mark-making, a device relevant less for sculpture than for the spontaneous remit of 'action' painting and for the fortuitous glazed firing techniques of 'Raku' in modern studio ceramics.

In this particular sense Kremer's soft, lush, pastoral vision is genuinely 'gartenbilden'. In common with Monet's late Giverny murals, Patrick Heron's 'Eagles Nest' abstractions, Ivon Hitchen's wide angle mid-Sussex panoramas and Alan Reynolds's Kent hop fields, Kremer alights on the source material of the garden, the forest or the open parkland. This has always figured in her 'oeuvre' from a series of vertical, axiomatically titled 'Garden' canvases made up from writhing strands of pure colour against stained backgrounds (1981-82) to the *'Hengistbury Head'* (2002), *'Highcliffe'* (2006) and *'Holton Lee Study'* series. In these instances the references to tall trees and to woodland themes becomes site specific and tied to place.

*3 Kremer's recent screen prints and monotypes were inspired by a series of screen printing courses with Liz Cotton at Poole Printmakers, founded by John Liddell in 1991.

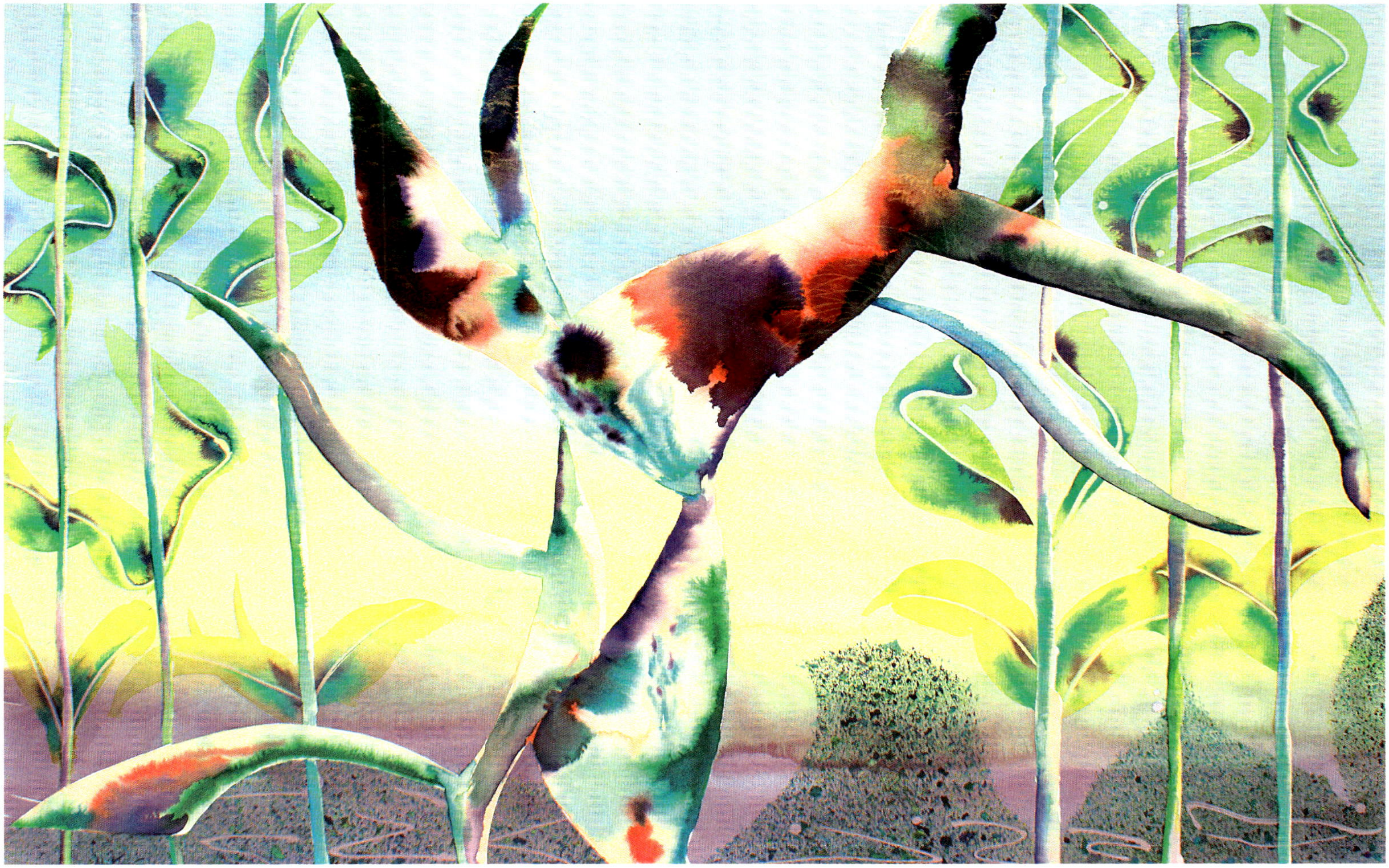

Highcliffe 2 2006
Watercolour
90cm x 125cm

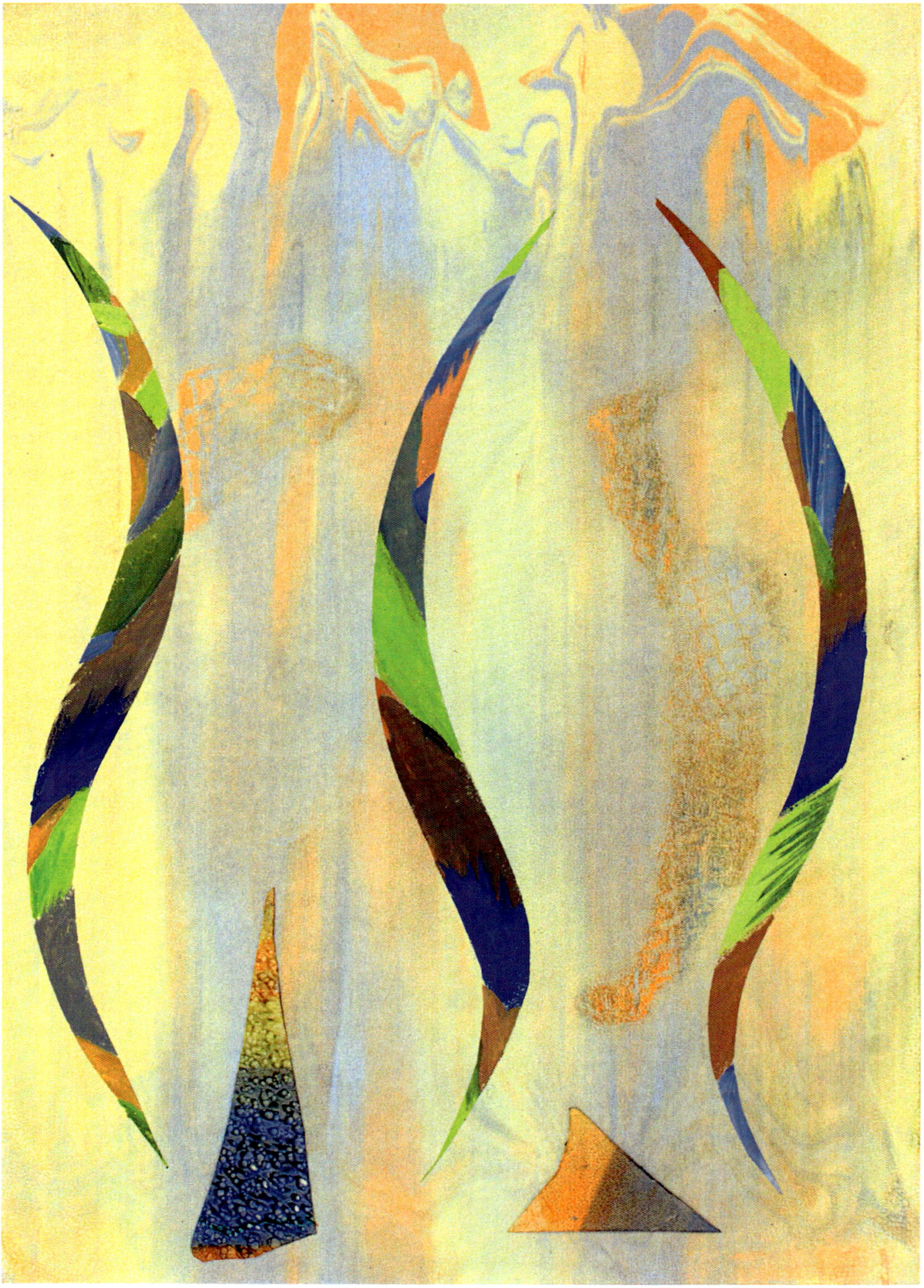

Holton Lee Print Series 1 No.6 2008
Mixed media mono screenprint
40cm x 25cm

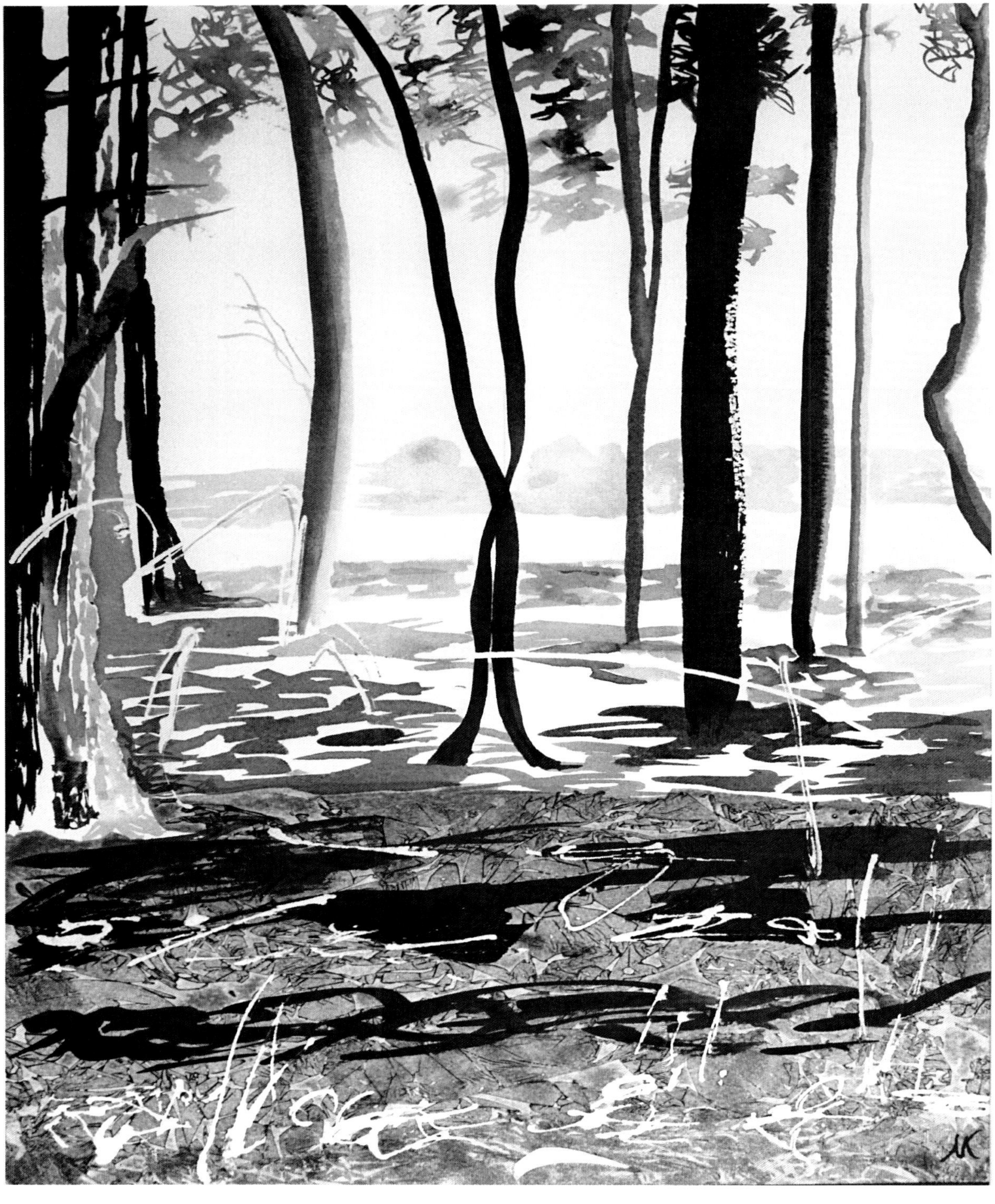

Holton Lee Study 1 2005
Indian ink on paper
45cm x 30cm

Abi Kremer

In Context

The tall pine trees running from Sandbanks and Poole Park through the Chines to Bournemouth and beyond are generic, as well as site specific, sources for Kremer compositions like the *'Woodland'* (1994) and *'Woodland Dance'* (2005-6) canvases or *'Treescape'* series (2008). The vertical tree trunk motifs fulfil both surface and perspectival functions and throughout there is a dichotomy between abstract and representational intentions, the one holding the other in check. But whereas gorgeously tinted earlier colour 'field' compositions like the *'Dancer'* series (1980), the *'Garden'* pictures and *'Summer Haze'* (1988) posited gestural lines or slashes of colour, with varying degrees of abstract significance or figurative association, against spare backgrounds, later works like the *'Element'* and *'Untitled'* series (2008) formalised gestural surface mark into distinct, multi-coloured and hard-edged 'boomerangs', or 'arcs'. This formalisation is symptomatic of Kremer's underlying abstraction. In contrast to Friedrich or early Mondrian, Kremer's forests are not dank primeval or theosophical symbols but rather breathe with the bright, dappled energy of light and colour, prismatically distributed among an arboreal architecture.

The human figure, moving and dancing, has provided an equally powerful source for Kremer's lyrical vision. The celebrated painter and printmaker Prunella Clough, a visiting tutor at Bournemouth College of Art in the mid 1970's soon after Kremer's *'Reflections'* had left the easel, saw an individual pictorial voice emerging capable of exploring salient experimental avenues. Another visitor, the analytical post-Euston Roader, Euan Uglow, saw a tastefulness in Kremer's loose handling and pale, melodious colour. Like good social manners this tastefulness provides Kremer's 'oeuvre' with a salutary and salubrious note, an idealism even, and runs counter to much later-day YBA 'anti' or 'bad' art. She makes no concessions to such deleterious distractions, upholding instead a few abiding principals of an ethical and aesthetic nature.

Another key student work *'Dancer Triptych'* (1976), a plaster relief with an aluminium powder finish was inspired by the Ballet Rambert. Interested in ballet since a schoolgirl in London, Kremer later made drawings of the ballet troupe at the Poole Arts centre now the Lighthouse, in the early 1980's from which she produced many dance paintings. This thematic material once again highlights the artist's taste for graceful movement and balletic posture. Dance has usually been of more relevance to sculpture, hence Kremer's one-off bas relief, but given this painter's perennial preoccupation with movement and flux, provides a wholly suitable source. In contrast to the foxtrot of the 1930's (which inspired Mondrian) or the 'twist' of the 1960's - dances associated with specific cultural and social eras – the ballet is timeless and classical and as such provides a purely formal source for the artist. The challenge of drawing rapidly from the performing figure fuels Kremer's inherent gesturalism, her characteristic speed of handling, and results in the 1979 *'Dancers'* series where the crit cal relationship between drawing and painting is also illustrated in terms of iconographic distillation and deployment of line as colour. In these instances Kremer's bridge between the plastic and performing arts rests not only on the dancer subject matter but on her notion of painting as a rapid performance in its own right.

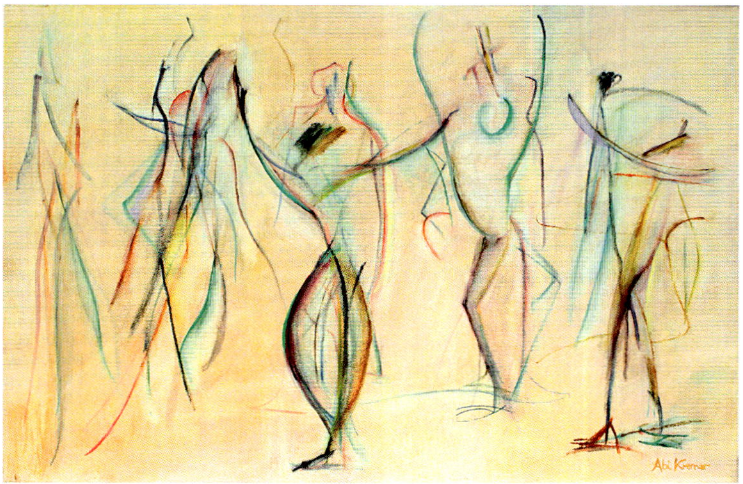

Dancers 1 1980
Oil on canvas
60cm x 90cm

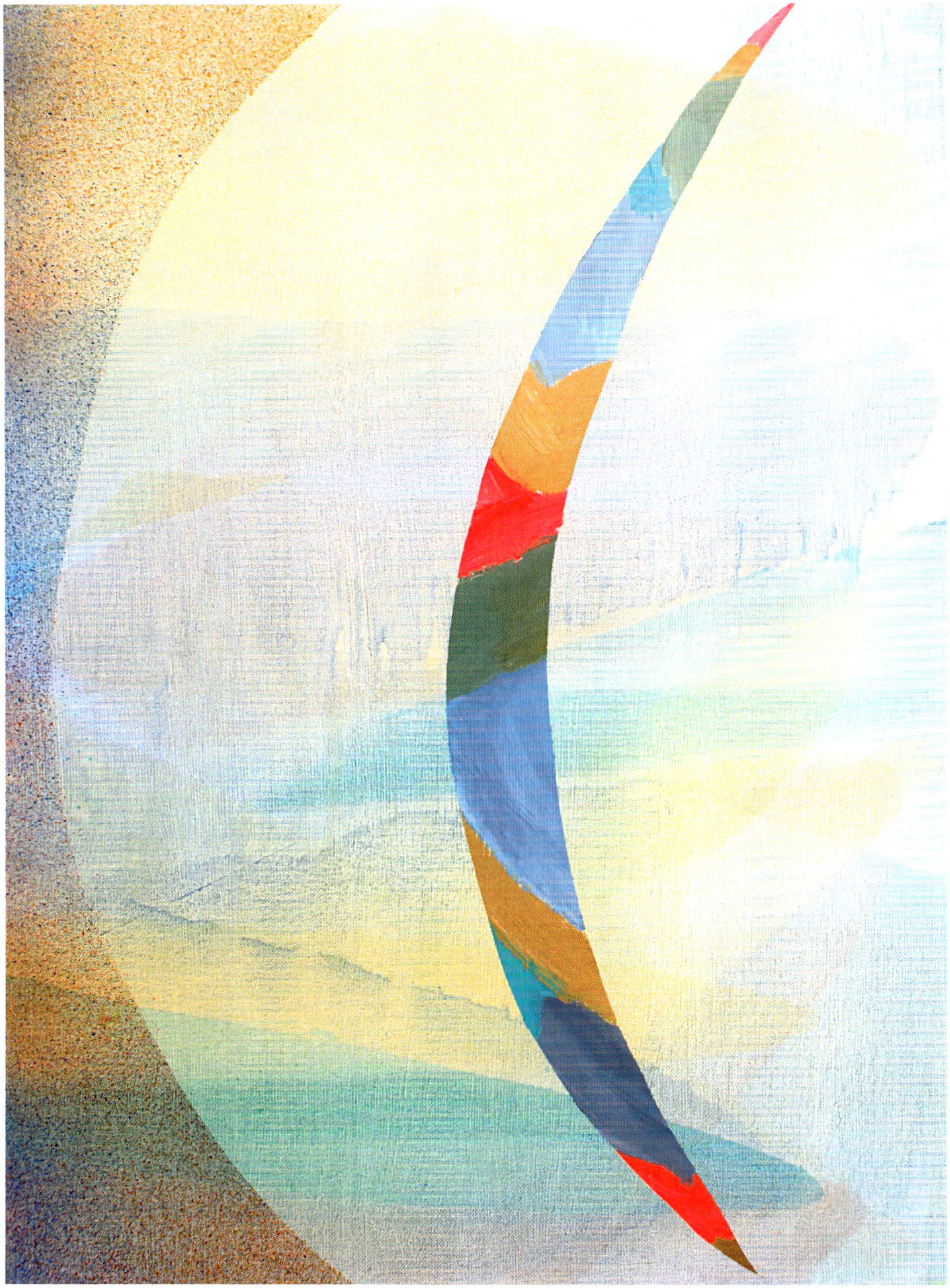

Untitled 4 2008
Oil on canvas
70cm x 50cm

Abi Kremer

In Context

Kremer's canvases are never cluttered and have an airy, even ethereal subtlety; on occasion the paint, as a fluid substance, does the work. In the *'Element 6'* (2008), for example John Hoyland-like paint runs define imagery of an almost palpable kind. The 'Zen' notion of 'less is more' is certainly at play, a factor that also hints at a probable understated spiritual dimension. Kremer's ongoing correspondence with the art critic Sister Wendy Beckett is indicative of this. The Norfolk-based nun was discovered by the critic Peter Fuller (1942-90) whose Marxian, atheist and modernist beginnings were subjected to a thoroughgoing revision in which nature and the romantic British landscape tradition was reclaimed. Contacting Kremer via the Poole Arts Centre after reading my 'Arts Review' report of Kremer's spring 1987 show, Sister Wendy told Kremer her work was "hauntingly beautiful" *4. Much later in response to the artist's 2005 drawing display at the Russell-Cotes the critic once again told the artist that "the graphic work has real poetry" *5.

Artists like Kandinsky, Mondrian, Newman and Rothko, have at the root of their work, a transcendentalism of purpose. Kremer would probably shy away from over-defined or doctrinaire positions but being the modern painter she is partakes of the same spiritual and musical preoccupations that have been a quiet but insistent part of the ethos of modernism over the last century.

Peter Davies

Peter Davies is a renowned Art Historian and author. Amongst his many publications are: "Art in Poole and Dorset", "Bratby", a series of art history books on St. Ives and most recently a biography of Marjorie Parr, Chelsea and St. Ives art dealer. He has contributed widely to national periodicals including the Independent and Arts Review.

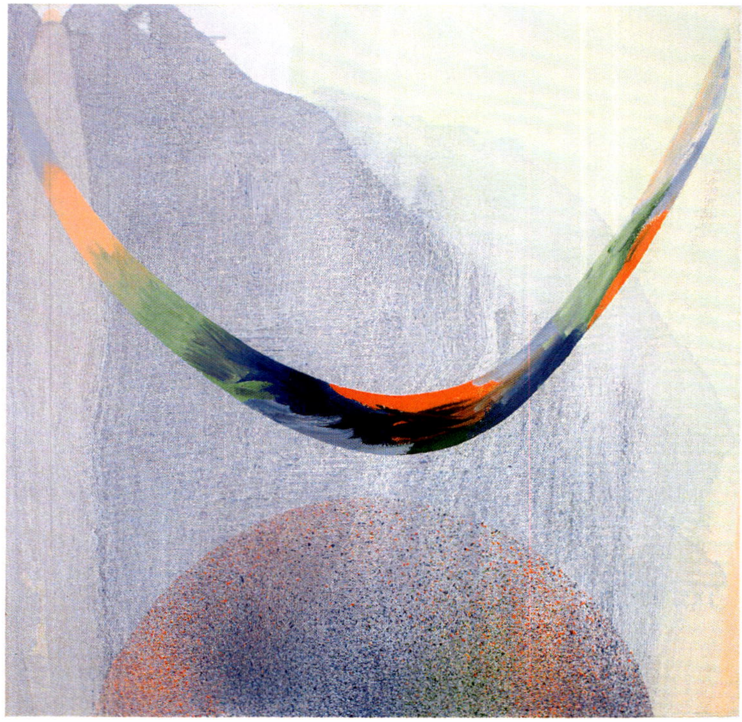

Element 5 2008
Oil on canvas
60cm x 60cm

*4 Sister Wendy Beckett to Kremer 3/6/87.

*5 Sister Wendy to Kremer 2005. My two 'Arts Review' reports on Kremer's Poole and Havant shows appeared in April 1987 and July 1989 respectively.

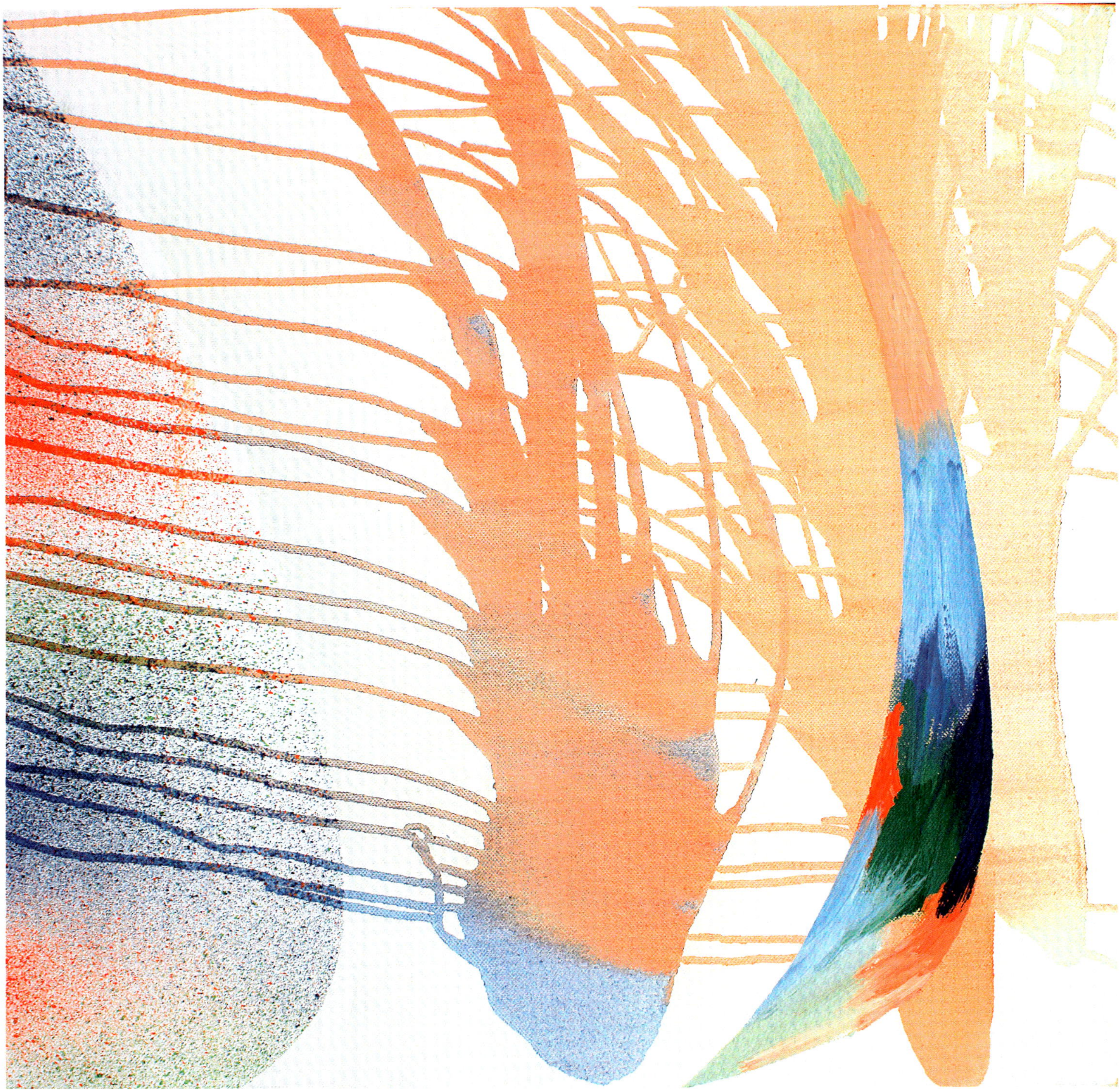

Element 6 2008
Oil on canvas
60cm x 60cm

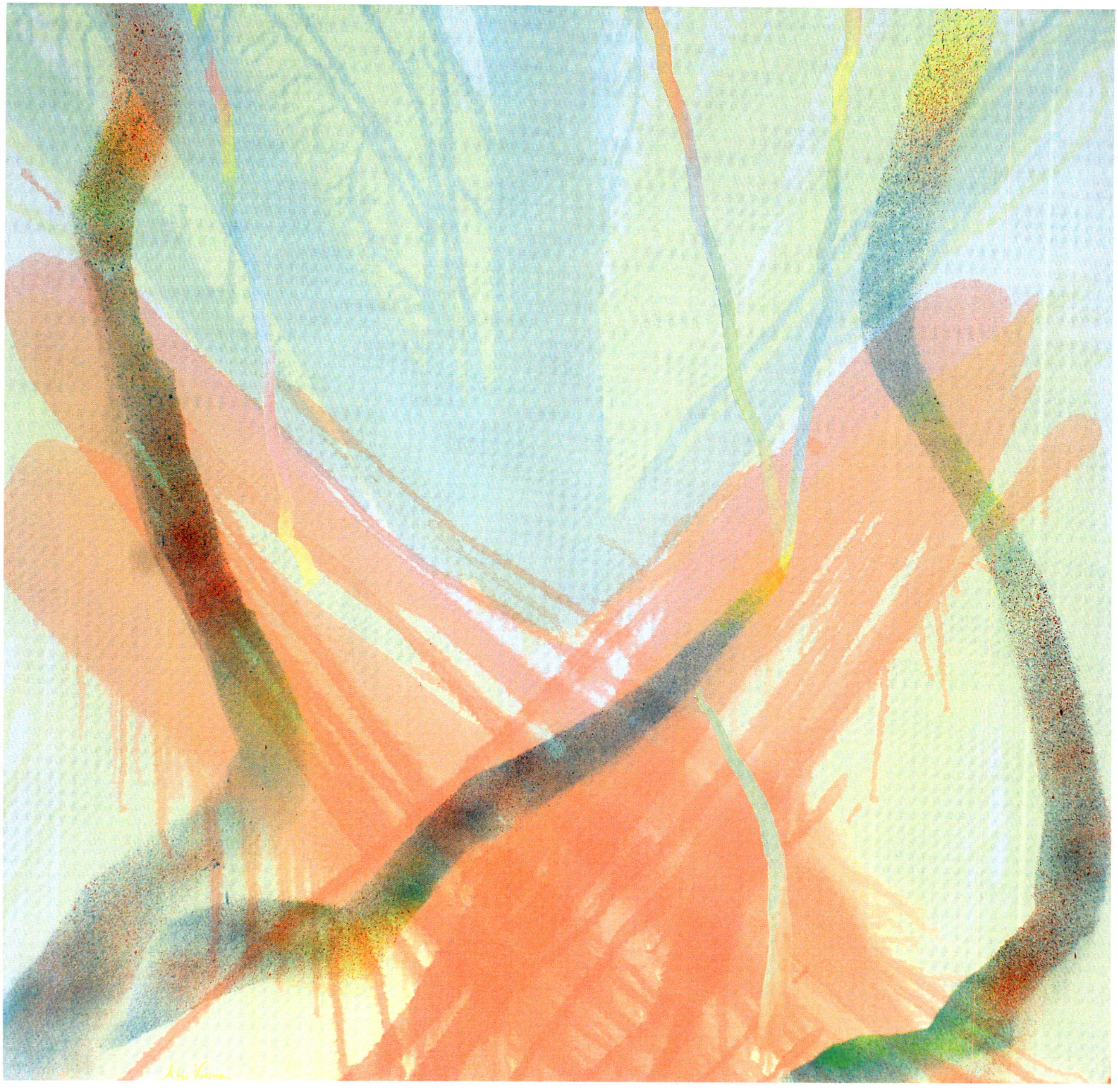

Woodland Dance 2 2006
Oil on canvas
90cm x 90cm

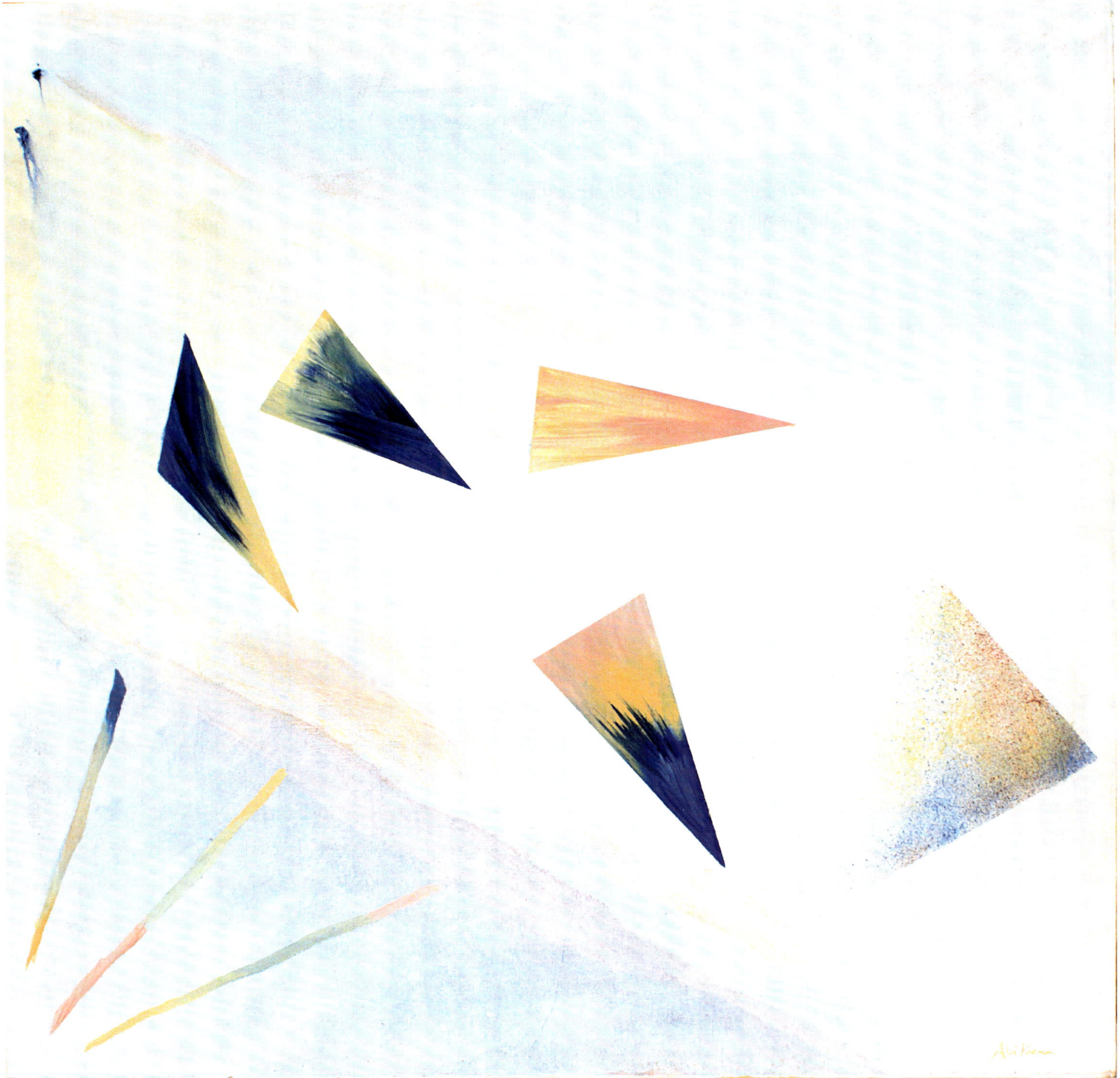

Lapis Lazuli 2005
Oil on canvas
90cm x 90cm

Abi Kremer

Colour and Inspiration

Abi Kremer is a well known and respected artist who has spent her 30 year career working in Bournemouth and Poole - exhibiting and selling work in many cultural, public and private institutions throughout the South West region. Her belief in the power of art to heal and transform everyday life has led to a rich variety of public art projects in Dorset, Hampshire and Wiltshire.
She continues to be a loyal colleague, supporter and friend, to many art and non-art public and private organisations in the UK. Her 17 year teaching career at Bournemouth and Poole College and Bournemouth and Poole Adult Learning is combined with commitments to individual projects.

Kremer is totally focused and disciplined about her art and teaching profession taking each responsibility seriously. Throughout her career she has made use of 'pockets' of time to develop her work; firstly as the demands of motherhood and family occupied her time and subsequently during her teaching years to push her work forward by experimenting and developing fresh ideas. Her term time activity to support students in developing their own work whilst expanding her knowledge of artists and their techniques continues to be a fundamental process in motivating her self direction. This publication is an opportunity to document her artistic practice as a whole, and to present the skill of painting as a refreshing medium at a pivotal point in her career.

Kremer's admiration of the artists Winifred Nicholson, Helen Frankenthaler, Paule Vézely and Bridget Riley - women who reflect a passion for and total commitment to their careers – reinforces her lifelong principle concerning the development of her work. Kremer has fought her own path to develop her ideas and practice, and it is the inspiration of artists such as these that continue to encourage her to produce vital and ever-changing new work.

Kremer has found particular empathy with the work of Winifred Nicholson, celebrated for her highly personalized impressionistic style inspired by nature, colour, landscape and spirituality. Her article *Unknown Colour* published in 1937 and a collection of letters that formed a dialogue with her friend the poet Kathleen Raine have been pivotal to Kremer's work, as they explore the relationship between music and colour as related abstract disciplines.

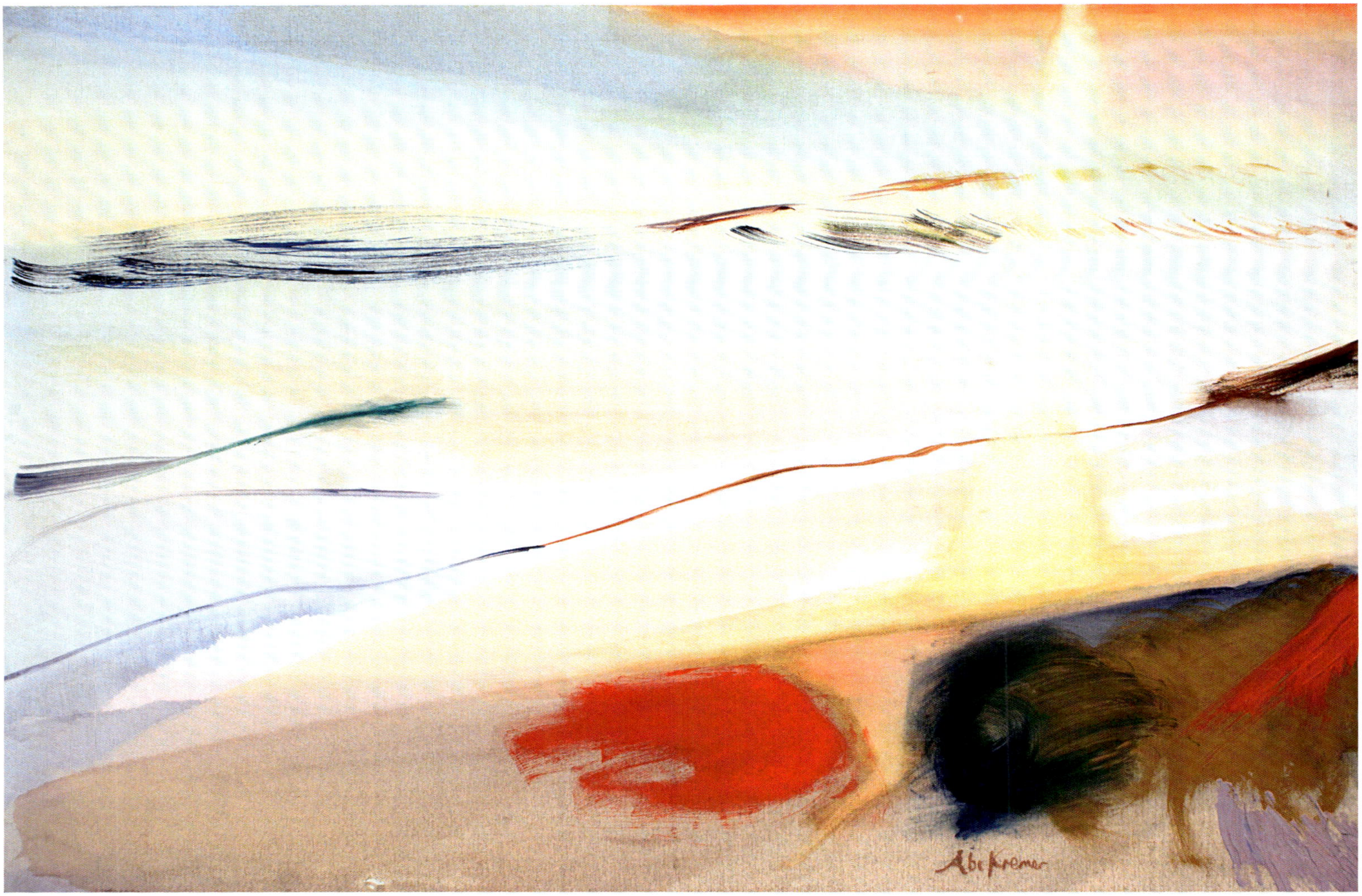

Sunset 1993
Oil on canvas
80cm x 120cm

Abi Kremer

Representational Work

Kremer's formative student years instilled the beginnings of a rigorous training in drawing and colour theory that has informed her career, resulting in a unique technique and style intertwiring colour, spirituality, the importance of music and sense of place. Her early paintings *Ostend, 1920's* (1975) depicting her grandparents on their honeymoon and *Welsh Hillside Chasm* (1975) reflect craftsmanship and the figurative and lyrical style related to early studies influenced by post impressionists such as Cezanne and Manet. Her move to abstraction is apparent as *Reflections* (1977) a large scale abstract landscape with an expressionistic air marks a period of experimentation with colour. Inspired by her studies of abstract expressionism, Kremer used accidental coloured impressions on a sponge as a starting point in the mark making to create fluid and subtle mixes of pastel colour.

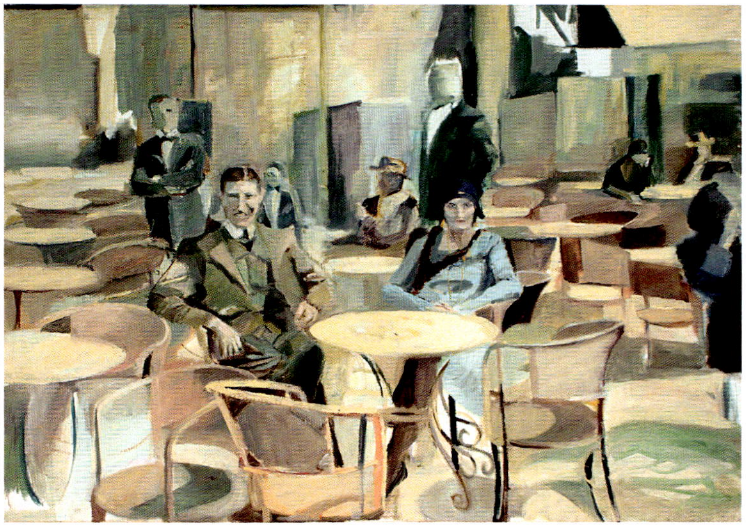

Ostend 1920's 1975
Oil on canvas
65cm x 90cm

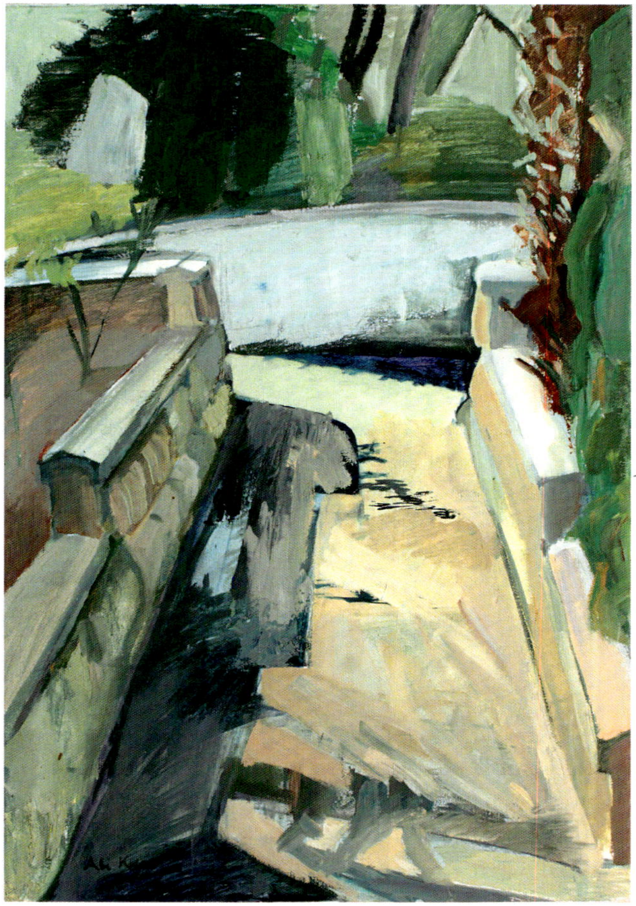

Pathway 1976
Oil on canvas
90cm x 60cm

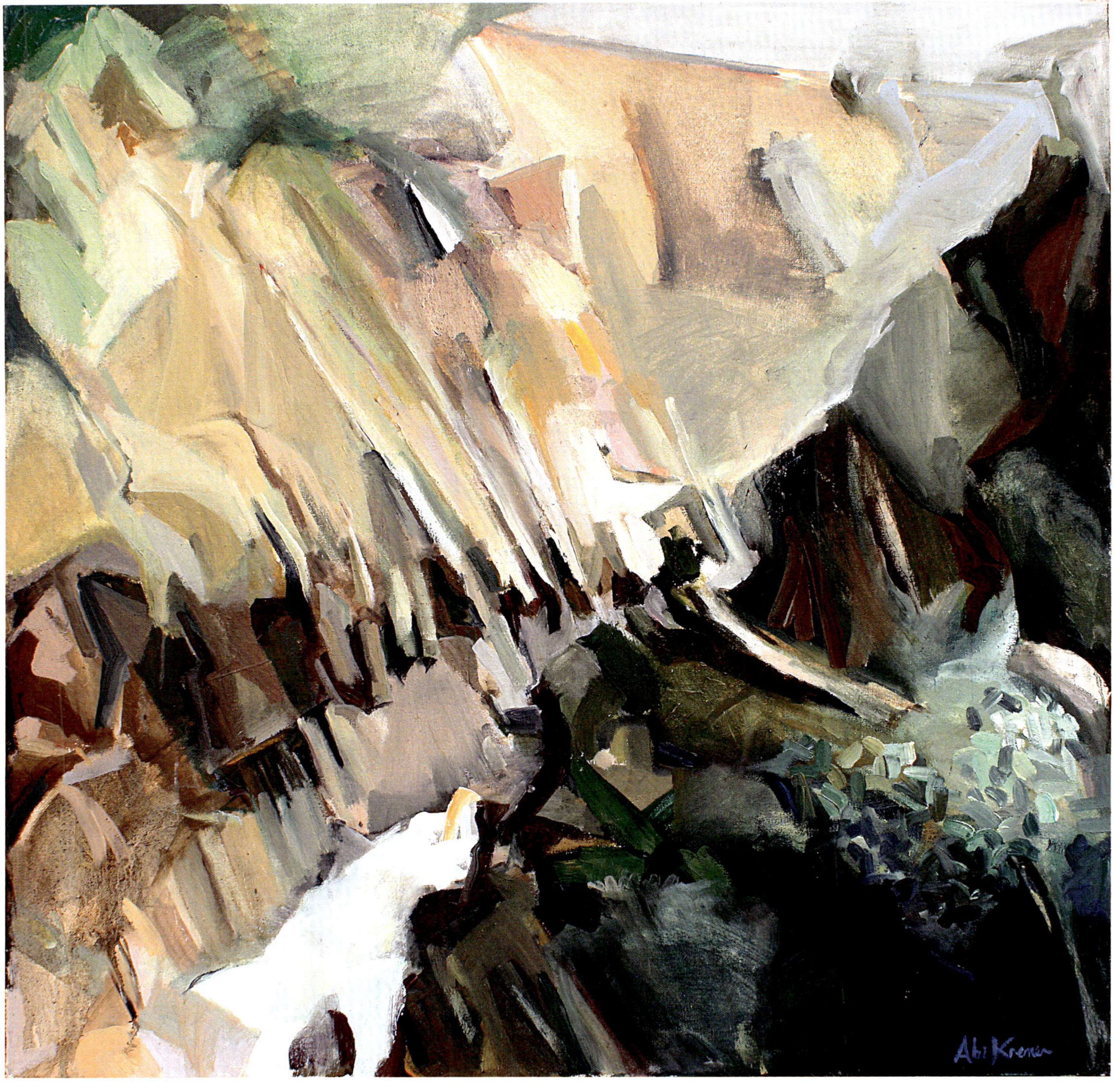

Welsh Hillside Chasm 1975
Oil on canvas
90cm x 90cm

Abi Kremer

Gestural Figure and Movement

Kremer's studies and sketches of the Ballet Rambert in 1977 depict the underlying structure and form of dancers exercising at the bar and rehearsing dance pieces. This interest in performance art added another dimension to her developing oeuvre. The *Dancers Triptych* (1977) illustrates her mastery of relief sculpture incorporating futurist elements and dance – a connection to her previous studies of Degas and Matisse. However her approach to the Rambert sketches (1978), working largely in graphite and pastels, became increasingly abstract and gestural with dynamic lines and strident colours conveying a sense of energy. The calligraphic calmness of *Dancers 3* (1979) also depicts lyrical movement with the emphasis on stylized shape and form.

Kremer's awareness of music and art has continued since her days at Art College listening to Miles Davis and jazz improvisation when working. In 1993 she collaborated with the newly formed Europa String Choir at the Russell-Cotes Art Gallery & Museum. The 'performance' painting to the rhythm of music with the movement of paint developed into a 'conversation' with The Europa's electric violin and guitar. "Europa's unique sound and repertoire, consisting mostly of original compositions reflect their diverse backgrounds as musicians. The music is rich in variation of colour and texture, sometimes simple and lyrical, with a Celtic folk influence, sometimes intricately polyrhythmic and at other times more stridently rock oriented, though often with a touch of Bartok". A series of works on paper was developed and these illustrations were used for 'the Starving Moon' one of the Europa's compact discs.

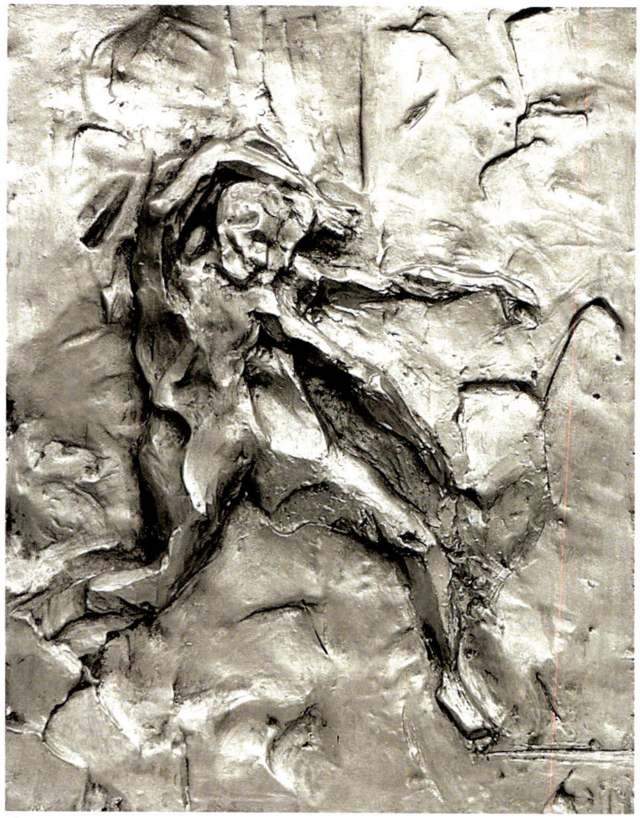

Dancer Triptych 1 1977
Aluminium powder on plaster
60cm x 45cm

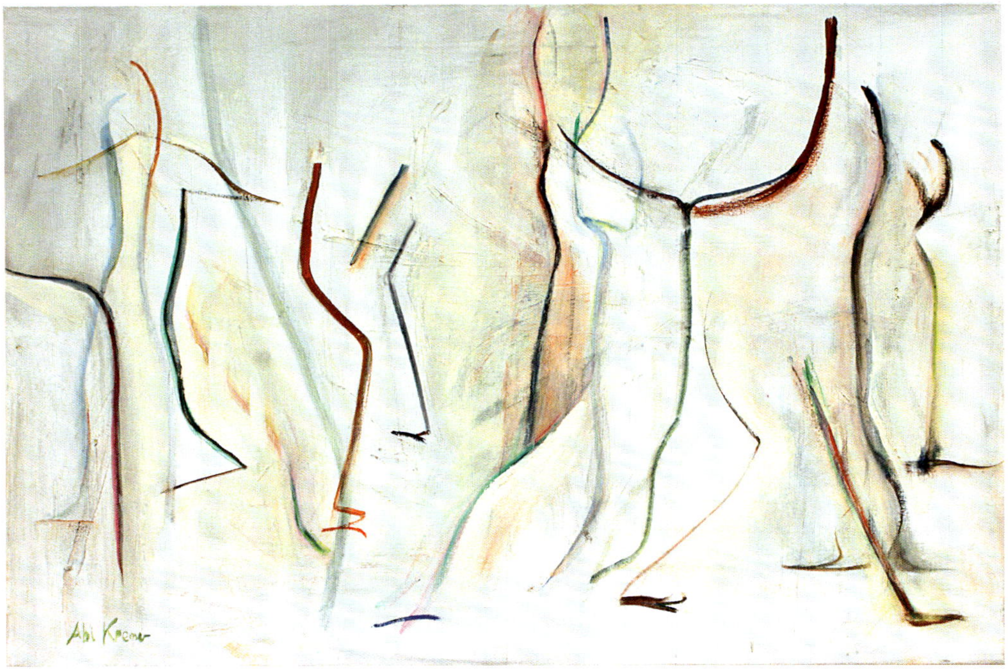

Dancers 3 1980
Oil on canvas
60cm x 90cm

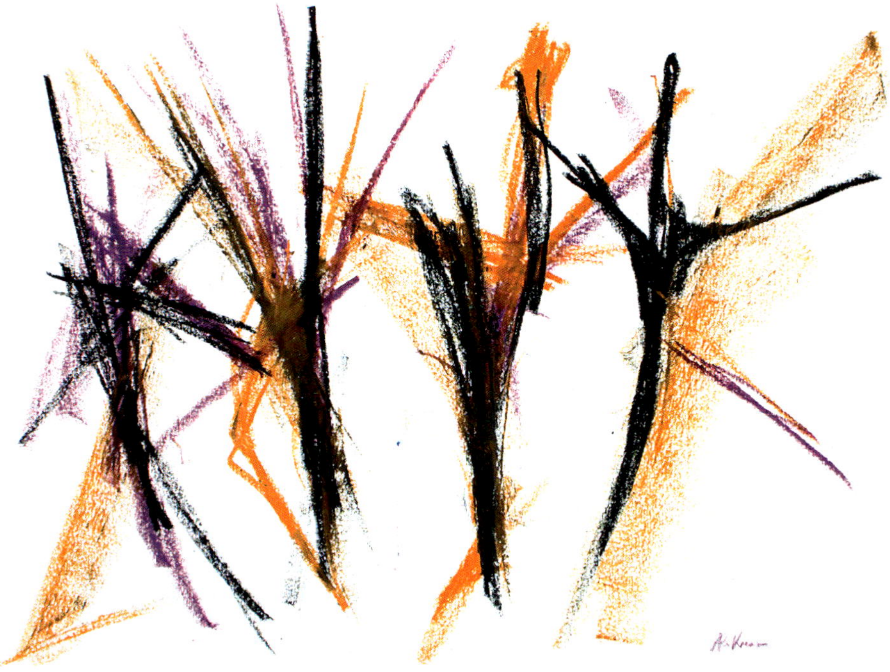

Rambert Sketch 5 1979
Pastel on paper
40cm x 55cm

Abi Kremer

Japanese Influences

At Art College Japanese Art and Zen philosophy with the aesthetic of minimal mark making (and her eventual thesis on Japanese Art) also influenced the direction of Kremer's work. The aesthetic of 'less is more' (making use of negative space) continues to be a strong dynamic and resonates in her work as much as the importance and discipline of concentrating on every brush stroke - meditating on composition and ideas and not overworking paintings.

Japanese Garden (1982) reflects Kremer's emerging style expressing spontaneity and emotional experience, with a freedom in mark making and a sensitive use of media. As then, the Japanese influence is evident and far reaching in Kremer's work and she has successfully employed a diverse range of media and techniques over the years. The elegant calligraphic brushstrokes of *Japanese Watercolour 2* (2005) and *Global Warming Monoprint No.2* (2007) are excellent examples of process.

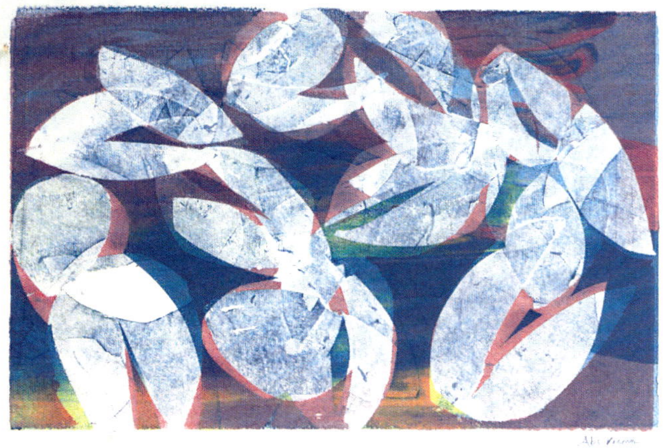

Global Warming 2 2007
Monoprint
15cm x 20cm

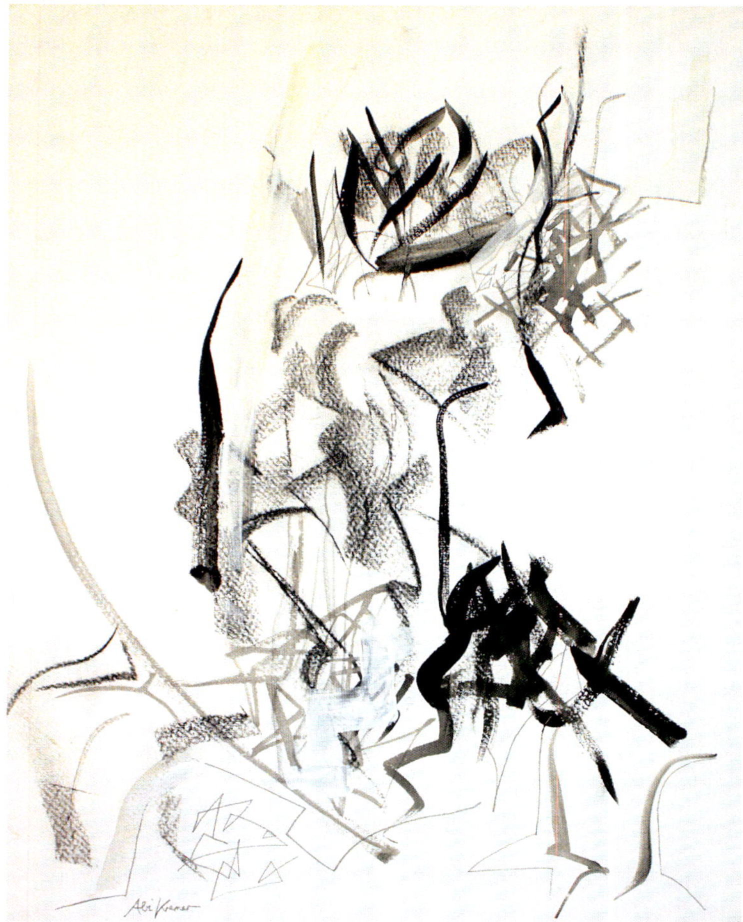

Japanese Garden 1982
Mixed media on paper
50cm x 40cm

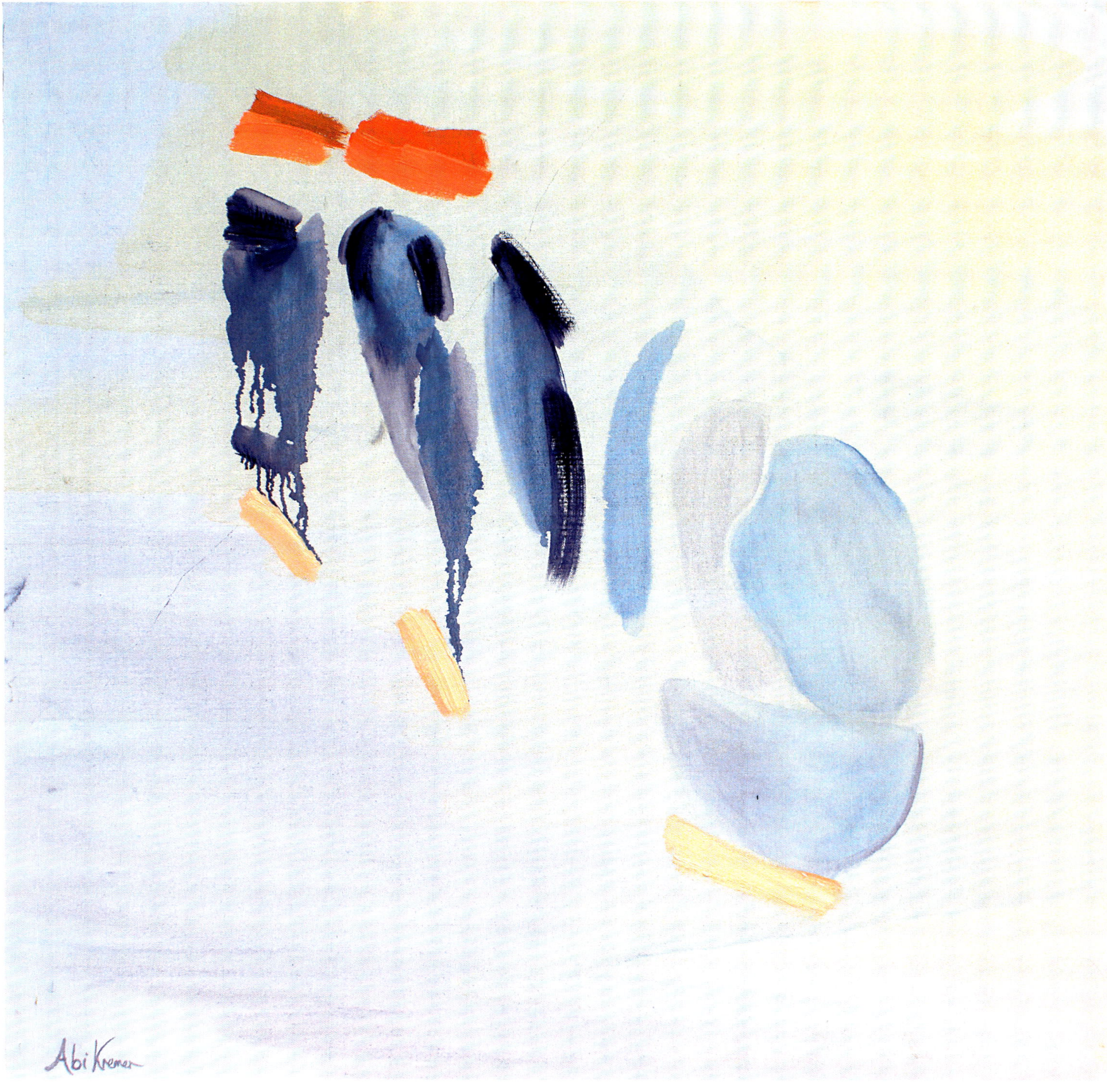

Flow 2 2002
Oil on canvas
100cm x 100cm

Abi Kremer

Commissioned work

Kremer's keen interest in environmental art also developed from her study of the Japanese aesthetic and it is here that she most importantly gained an understanding of sense of place. Her love of nature and discipline of working to a brief furthered her emerging practice at the end of the 1970's, which led her to seek opportunities to create large scale site specific work. Early opportun ties were limited to a commission on a restaurant boat 'The Tom Pudding' and a Viking ship relief; however Kremer's desire to create work for specific spaces where the public could view and enjoy it later resulted in many public commissions in youth centres, libraries, schools and local hospitals. Of these works it is difficult not to be charmed by the *Millennium Baby Hand Print Ceramic Panel,* commissioned by Bournemouth Hospital in 2000 which depicts the number of infants born from January to December of that year. The gynaecological unit at Bournemouth hospital commissioned a series of work for treatment rooms in 1995, resulting in a series of delicate almost ethereal studies of nature on a selection of refreshing mauve, green and yellow hued canvases. *Headlight 3* (2000) is one of a series of paintings commissioned for Christchurch Stroke Rehabilitation Unit that provide hope and inspiration to patients in recovery, with an uplifting colour palette using oil washes to represent the qualities of light and space at Hengistbury Head nearby. The Past Rotarians Club of Bournemouth commissioned a delicately painted glass leaf panel to commemorate the Golden Jubilee (1952-2002) of H.M. Queen Elizabeth II, which hangs in the lobby of the contemporary Bournemouth library building.

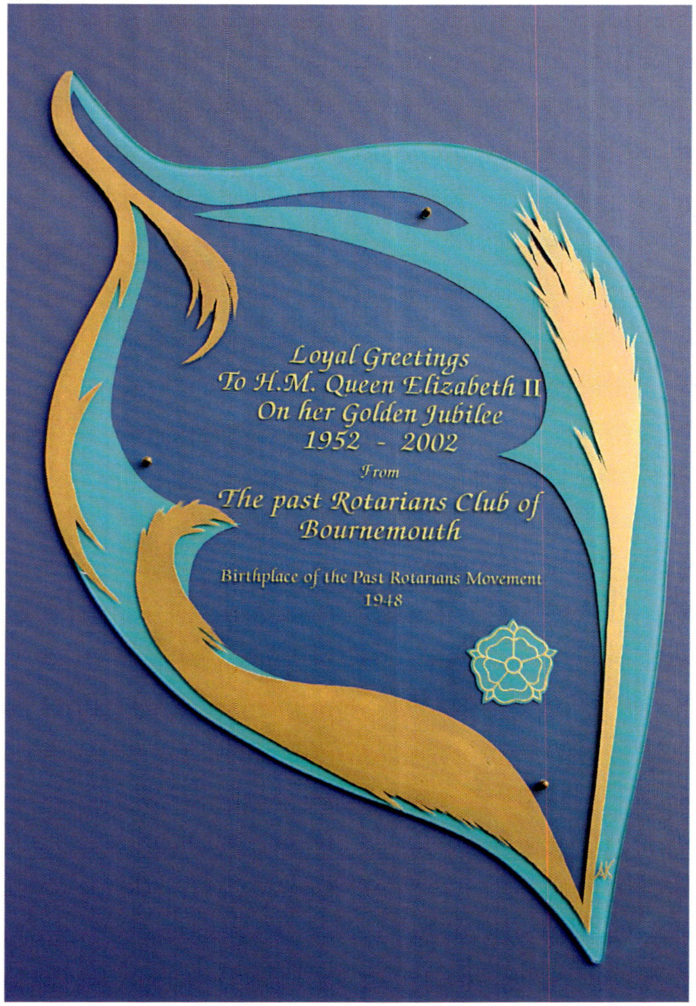

Bournemouth Library Golden Jubilee 2002
Printed glass
180cm x 120cm

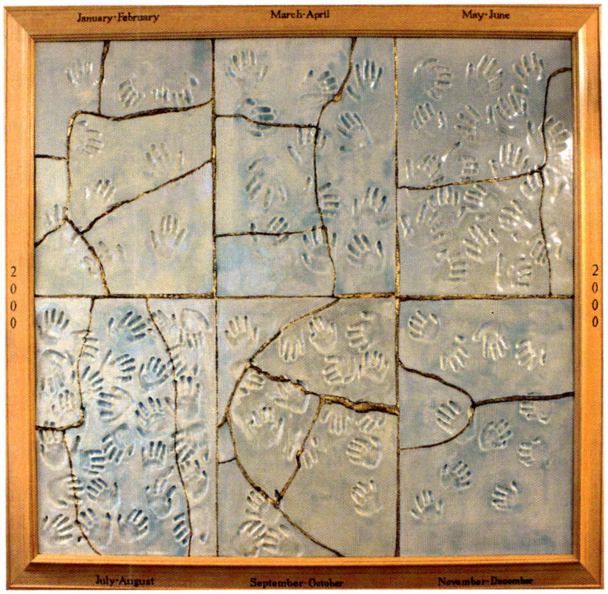

Millennium Baby Handprint Ceramic Panel 2000
Ceramic panel

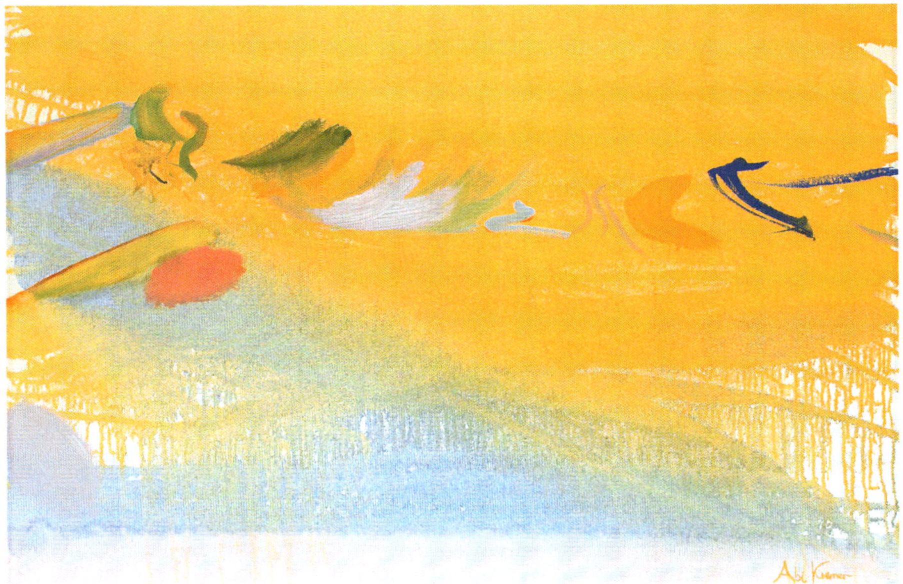

Headlight 3 2000
Oil on canvas
60cm x 90cm

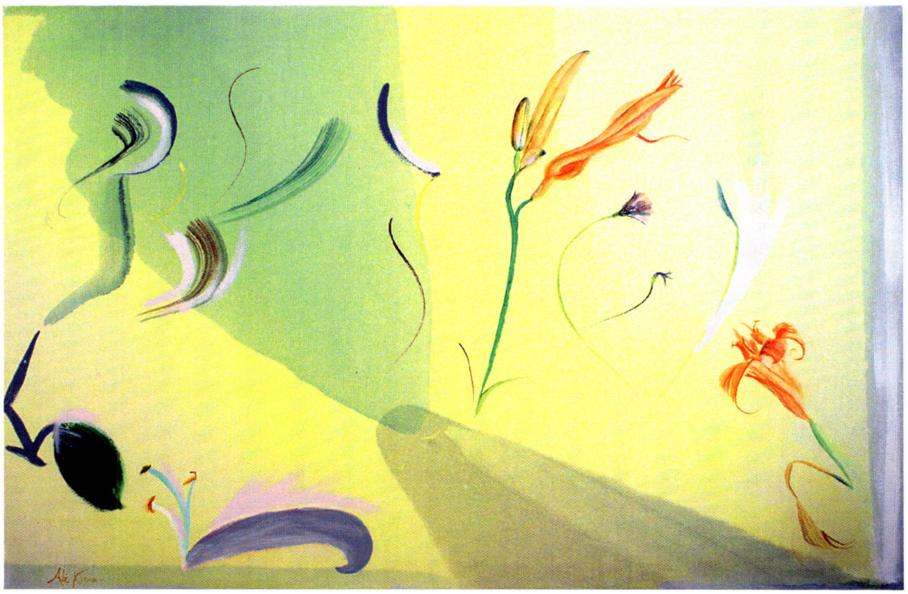

Flower Piece 1 Royal Bournemouth Hospital 1996
Oil on canvas
80cm x 120cm

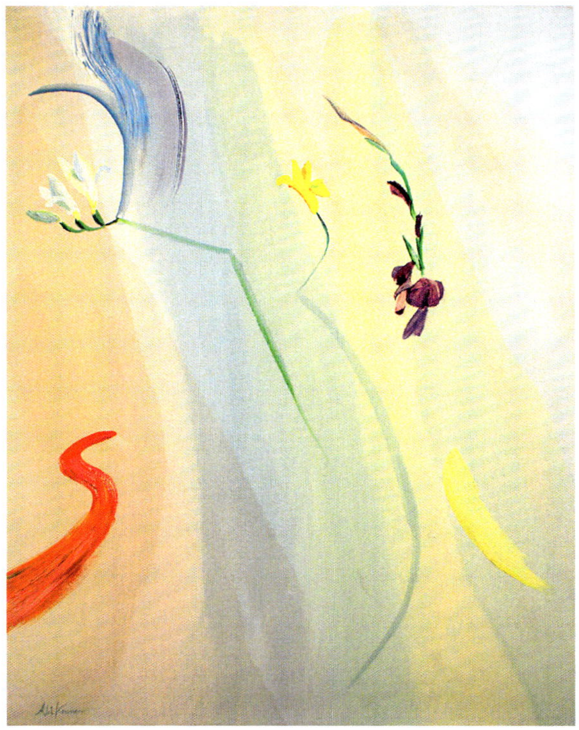

Flower Piece 3 Royal Bournemouth Hospital 1996
Oil on canvas
80cm x 60cm

Abi Kremer

Gestural Landscape Painting

The popular Dorset landscape has featured strongly in Kremer's work symbolizing the emotional, mythic and spiritual content characterized by highly personal gestural and painterly application, derived from a sense of place. Her work conveys a visual reference to colour as the focus, experimenting with transparency and opacity to create a meditative yet dynamic set of harmonies.

The Trio of paintings *Garden 1, Garden 2, and Garden 3* (1981-1982) have very strong expressionist elements deriving from initial graphic studies of nature. *In Garden 1* the lilac colour hints at figures dissolving towards the light; *Garden 2* represents tranquillity and in the case of *Garden 3* a bolder response makes use of thicker gestural marks. This connects with *Corfe Archway* (1987) emphasizing forms and structures evident in the landscape.

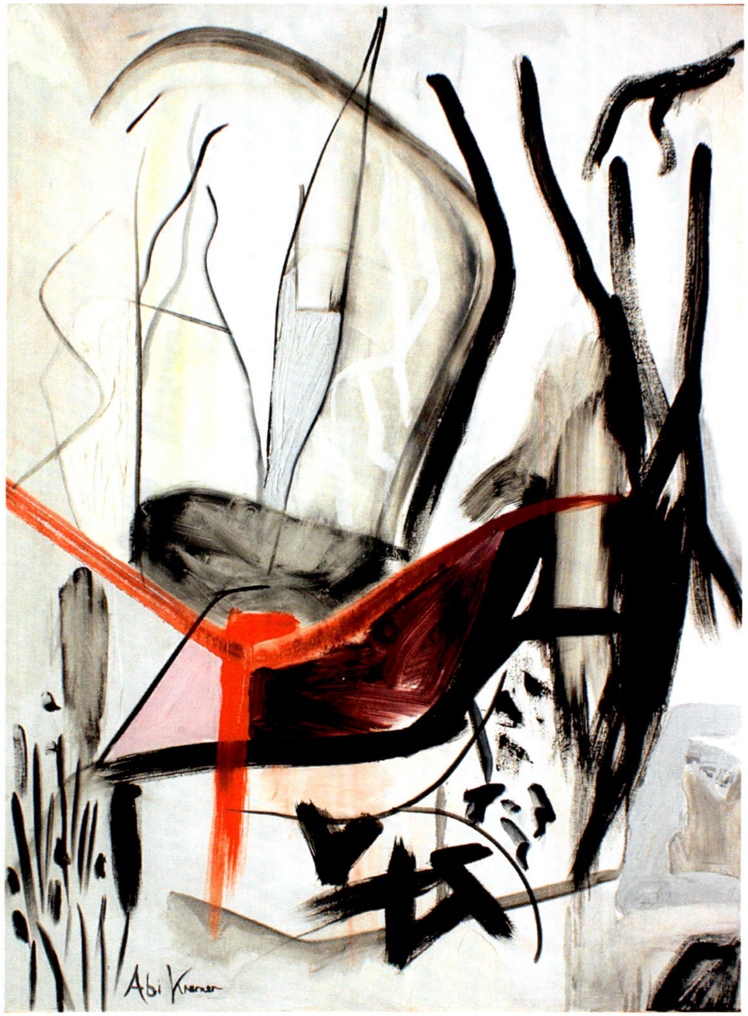

Garden 3 1982
Oil on canvas
150cm x 105cm

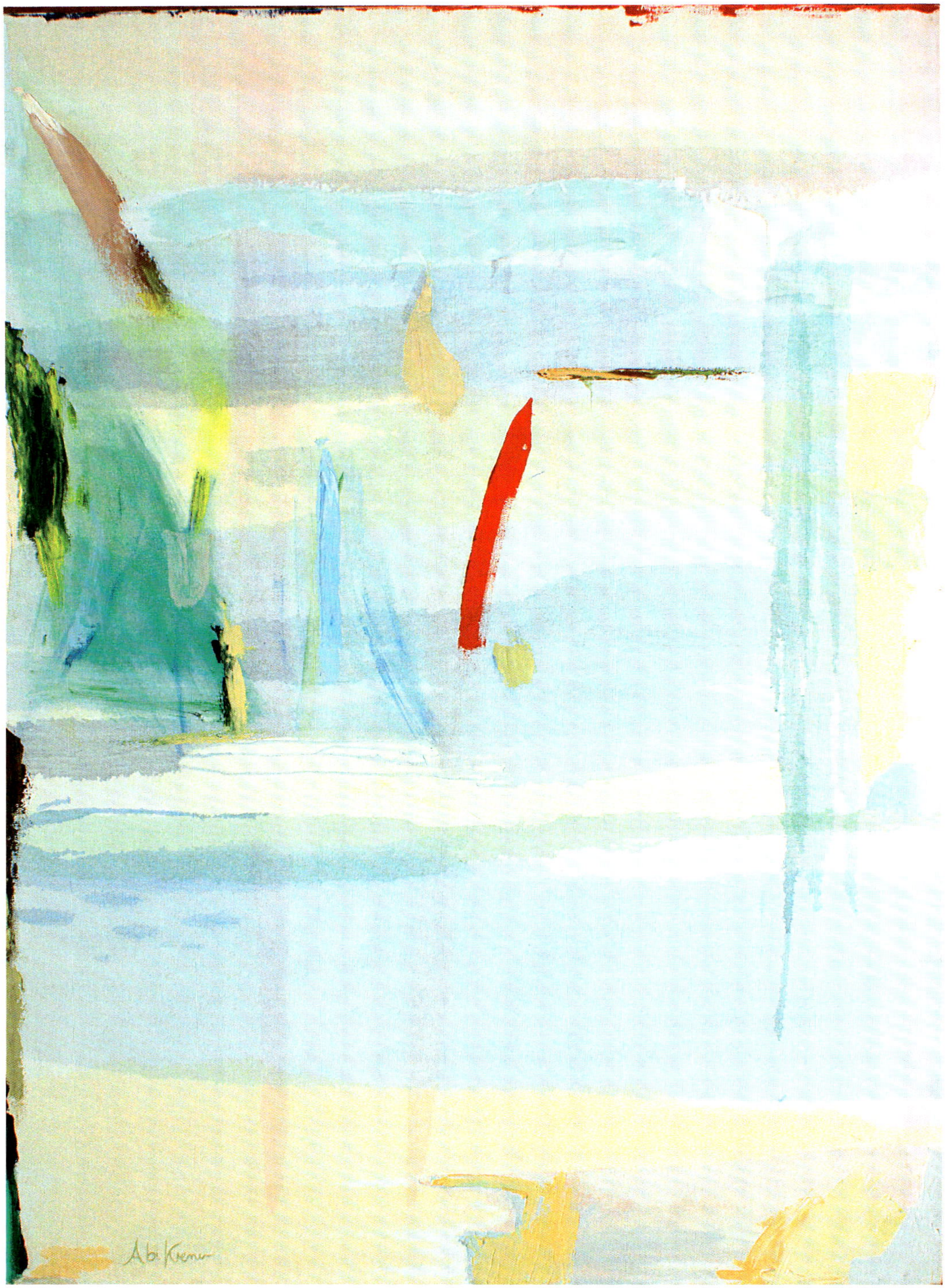

Garden 2 1981
Oil on canvas
150cm x 105cm

Abi Kremer

Lyrical Landscape

As Kremer's work developed she began to explore the relationship between landscape, music and dance and exploit this interest to develop a rhythm within mark making. The Paintings *Sea Mist, Storm Wind and Sunset* (1993) are excellent examples of this as they demonstrate the contemplative; forceful and tranquil qualities of the sea close to Bournemouth Pier and the qualities of fading light at dusk along the beach. Colour composition is really strong with a vivid and confident balance of warm reds, oranges and cool blues; the brush strokes on these landscapes are evidence of Kremer's colourist and craftsmanship qualities. *Sunset* with its subtle calligraphic brushstrokes conveys an ambience and transition of movement within the landscape. The top left of the painting depicts gradients of subtle blue and the bottom right beautiful brushstrokes of red, ochre and Prussian green. The composition of the landscape matures with subtle horizontal brushstrokes and gestures that draw the viewer into the landscape punctuated by explosions of colour, especially at the bottom right where the red balances the painting and provides a culminative point for the eye.

Sea Mist has a strong horizontal composition with more diagonal movement and contrasting gradients of orange and purple washes contrasted with blue and purple paint. The diagonal takes the eye from the bottom left of the painting with its blues and purples to the top right which is transparent and it is this musical movement of brushstrokes that enhances the composition of the painting.

Storm Wind is a mature composition of bold brush strokes of blue and brown thicker pigment on gentle washes of ethereal blue and green that signifies a balanced transition; the lamp posts in the distance also provide a vertical counterpoint to the painting adding depth and space.

These works were first exhibited in 'The Land and the Sea' Exhibition at the Russell-Cotes Art Gallery & Museum in 1993 and *Sea Mist* was acquired for the Museum's contemporary painting collection.

The Russell-Cotes Art Gallery and Museum, a Victorian seaside villa that stands proudly on the East Cliff of Bournemouth overlooking the Bay has been a constant source of inspiration for Kremer and her students. Formerly the home of Sir Merton and Lady Annie Russell-Cotes, its ambiance, décor and eclectic collections have created a wealth of subject matter for projects both inside the grade 2* listed building and in it's restored Victorian Garden. Kremer has been a loyal friend and supporter of the Museum and can often be found with a drawing class in the building or its grounds, supporting and guiding her students, as she constantly challenges them to look beyond the ordinary and continue to develop their work.

The watercolour *Hebe with Grotto, Russell-Cotes* (2004) was executed in the open air or 'en plein air'. It depicts the classical statue Hebe, amongst the foliage covered trellised archways and winding paths of the Russell-Cotes garden as she stands dignified amongst the forest of green interspersed with red and purple plants and flowers.

In recent years Kremer has produced a series of work from the surroundings of Highcliffe and amongst these two impressive colour landscape studies *Highcliffe 1* and *Highcliffe 2* (2006) stand out. Executed with ink wash to emphasise the stillness and depth of the background and calligraphic ink to highlight the depth and foreground detail, these works represent a transitional period drawing on Kremer's Japanese and surrealist influences, marked by the uniformity of colour and rhythm of the landscape.

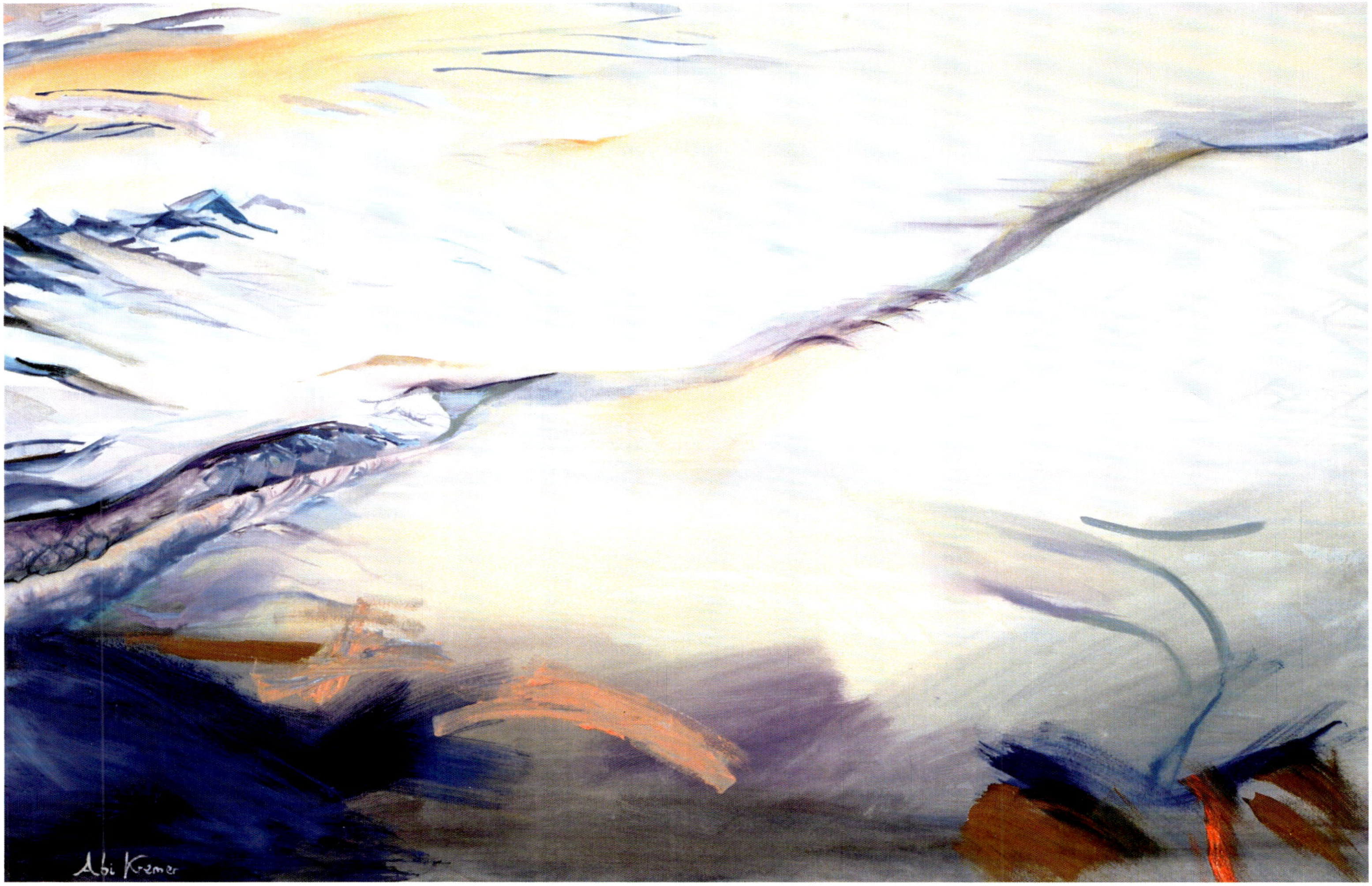

Sea Mist 1993
Oil on canvas
80cm x 120cm
courtesy of Russell Cotes Art Gallery and Museum

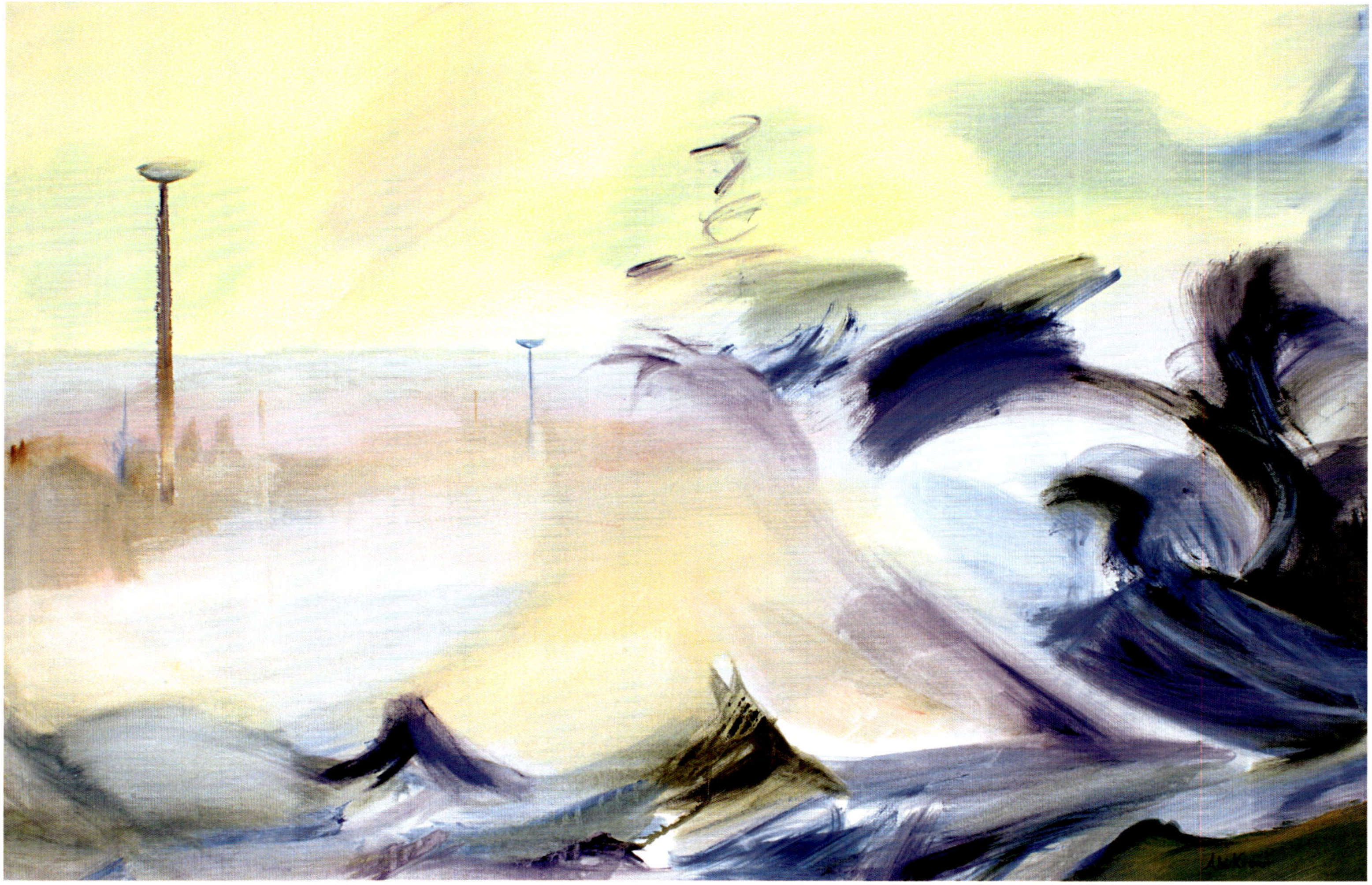

Storm Wind 1993
Oil on canvas
80cm x 120cm

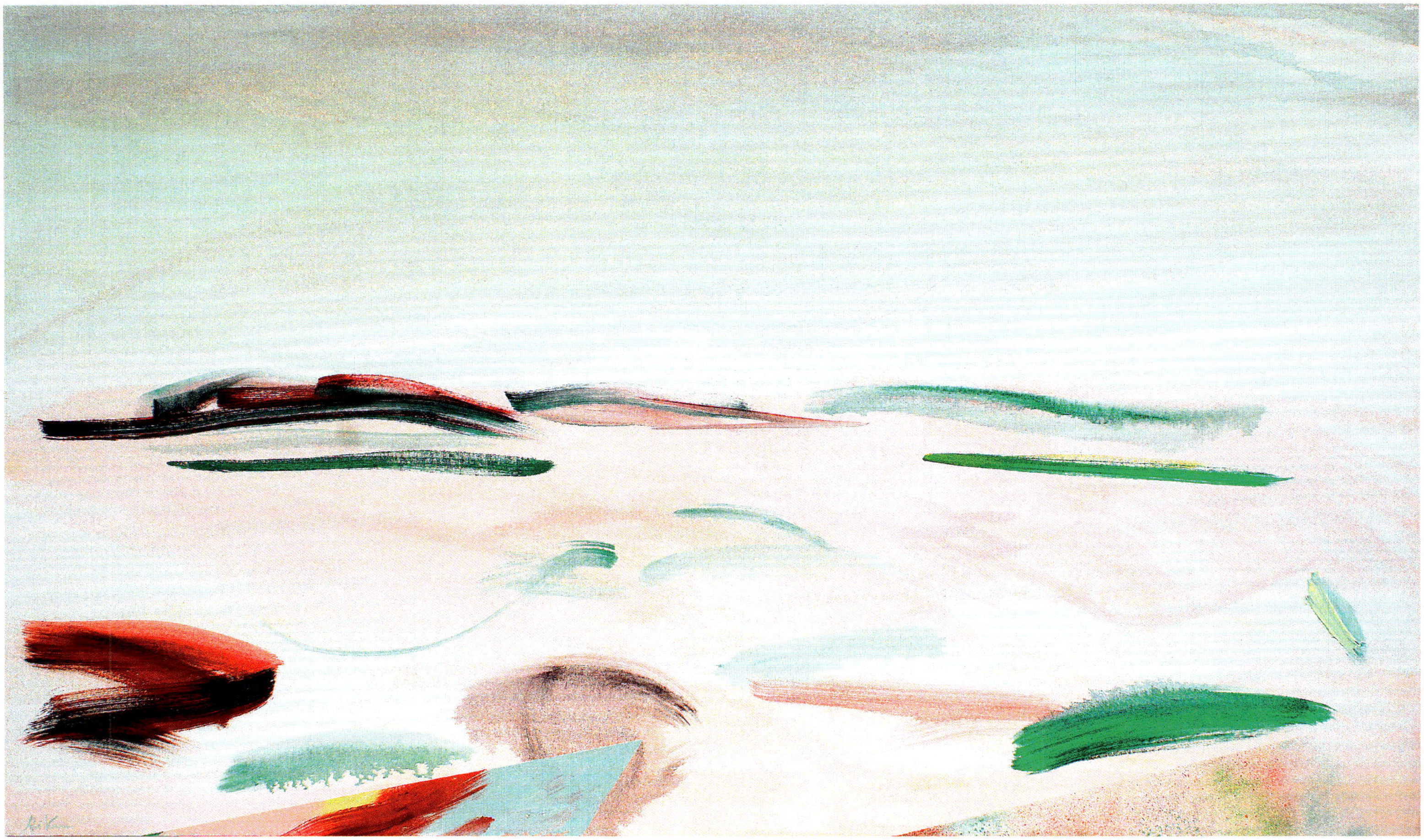

Current 2005
Oil on canvas
90cm x 150cm

Abi Kremer

Holton Lee

The impressive woodland at Holton Lee, East Holton on Poole Harbour is recognised as a Site of Special Scientific interest (SSSI); the Holton Lee landscape covers over 350 acres with a variety of habitats which include heath land, salt marsh, and reed bed. Its conservation of the habitat incorporates accessible pathways and resting places. Founded in 1993 by Faith Lees; Holton Lee offers holistic respite for those who are disabled, embracing physical, psychological, emotional and social care, encouraging personal growth, creativity and spirituality. Faith House, an architecturally renowned gallery, offers contemplative, social and cultural experiences.

Kremer has captured the tranquillity and intimacy of the habitats through studies, sketches and photographs; and these demonstrate her many years of experience of artistic process. The composition of *Holton Lee Study 1* (2005) becomes strongly vertical as Kremer successfully uses the lighting and interplay of horizontals and verticals. This is reinforced by *Woodland Sketch* (2009) with these elements counterbalancing to make a musical composition demonstrated by the trunks of the trees. The line of the horizon in the background and the long shadows of the trees also betray the time of the day captured by the evening sun, a moment in time, revealing a mature response to the subject matter.

Holton Lee Study 2 (2005) again represents a strong composition of the tree verticals and the long horizon of the landscape, in addition to the texture of the heathland and the beautiful washes of the sky. It is evident that the verticals of the tree trunks dominate the composition at the top half of the painting but are balanced by the horizontals depicting the forest floor and grasses providing texture at the bottom of the painting. These textures nicely juxtapose with the leaves in the upper part of the painting which is counterbalanced by the vacant area at the centre of the painting.

An Arts Council England grant was awarded to Kremer to develop this work as an Artist in Residence in 2006 which culminated in a Dorset Art Weeks show with fellow artist Richard Jeffrey. Working from Studio 1 at Holton Lee, Kremer's experimental ideas and techniques have steadily developed to produce the abstract *'Element'* series (2008), and colourful Holton Lee Print series that are strongly related to Kremer's previous figurative work at Holton Lee. These works represent the relationship of forms from nature i.e. the surface of a pond, patterns of vegetation, and the qualities of light and movement evident in the landscape. Kremers unique insignia is represented by experimenting with the visual language of colour, giving rise to the electric feeling of forms. Kremer has exploited filtered mark making and print making techniques using stippling, calligraphic inks, oils and print media, to capture the texture, depth, and the translucent qualities of her surroundings. Akin to the textile designs of Sonia Delaunay, Kremer's printing features strong abstract elements with colours allowed to run revealing the composition formed with layering, masking and mark making.

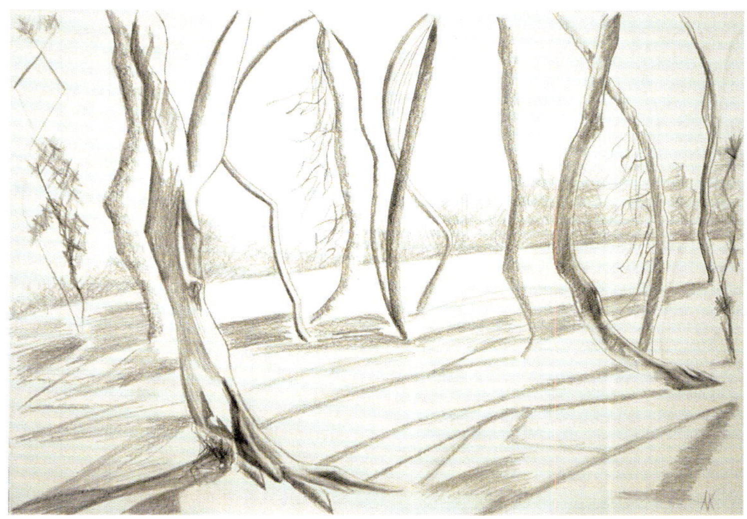

Woodland Sketch 1 2009
Graphite on paper
40cm x 60cm

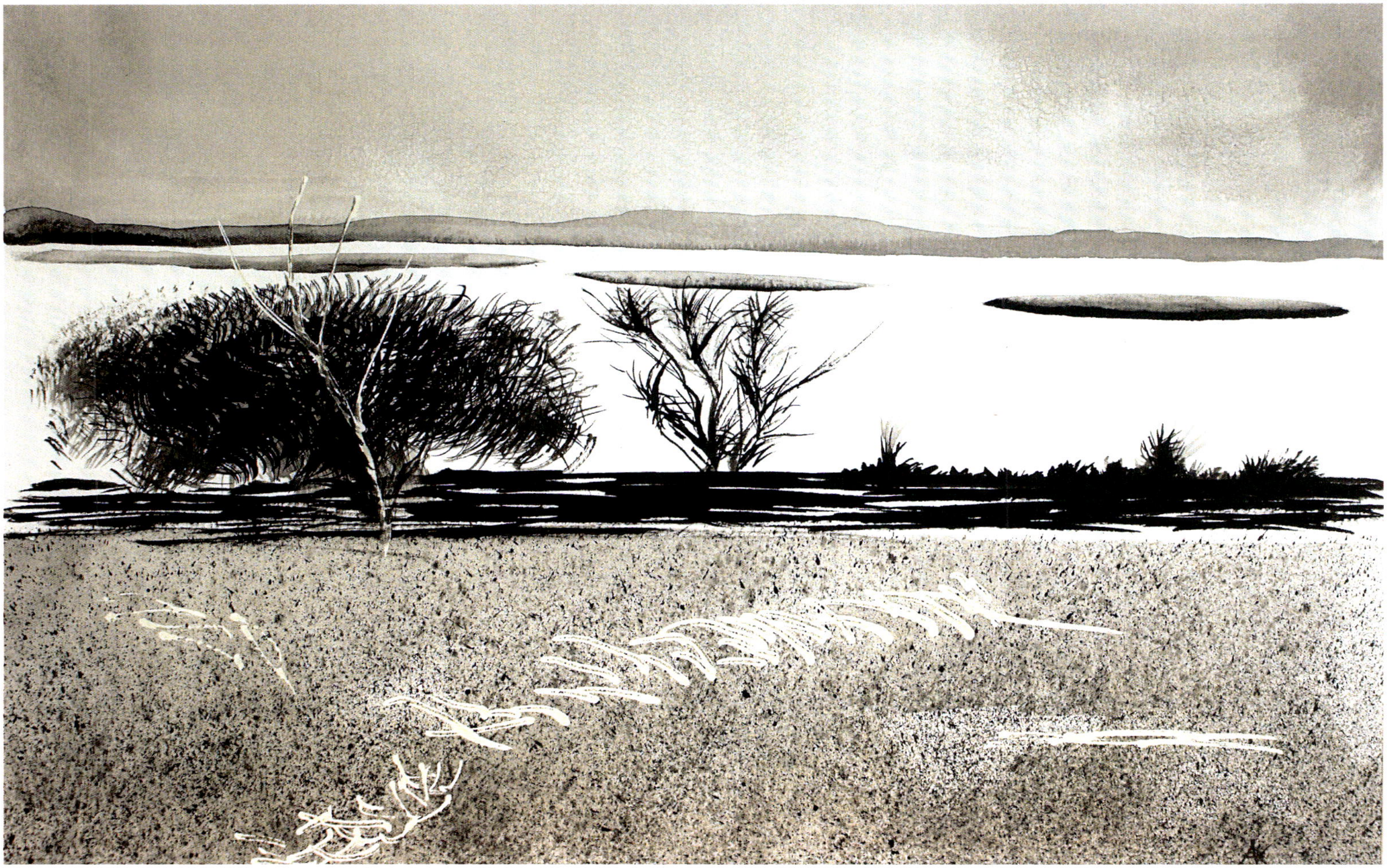

Holton Lee Study 1 2005
Indian ink on paper
45cm x 30cm

Abi Kremer

Holton Lee cont'd

The *Treescape* series is an apotheosis of colour. *Treescape 2* has superb gradients and bleeding of colour. Its strong vertical orderly movement of colour can be contrasted with a noisy gestural element that depicts the forest floor at the bottom of the painting. It possesses a surrealist and dream like quality, a mature colour composition that reveals years of experience and practise. The sense of movement and vibrancy re-emerges in *Treescape 3* (2008) - a lyrical magical composition represented by an explosion of inks. The strong vertical lines of the tree trunks give rise to the eruption of ink marks, counterbalanced by the deep warm velvet of the foliage at the top of the tree (left), which is simultaneously balanced by the pyrotechnic deep green foliage of the top right, showing perfect colour harmony and composition. An interchange of colour unfolds using a contrast of intensities between the two trees; the brown tree trunk balanced by green foliage and the green tree trunk topped by brown foliage. The shapes of the trees are mainly vertical, but caressed by the curved branches of the trunks. The scratchy multicoloured inks give additional texture to the composition of the trees culminating in a riot of colour on the forest floor.

Kremer's latest work combines printmaking and masking techniques with her painterly landscape style. In the background soft washes and gradients remind us of her lyrical landscape work. In the foreground Kremer uses abstract geometric elements instead of the representational landscape motifs of trees or sea. These geometrical elements, and others which are more organic, seem to float on top of the landscape background. The interesting development here is that the abstract forms seem to interact and counterbalance each other as if they are 'flocking' or 'floating' in tightly organised formations. Inside the geometrical forms Kremer has used bold gestural brush strokes and strong contrasts of colour – incongruent to the subtle variations of the background. *Emerald Movement* (2009) is an excellent example of this technique. In this instance the organic foreground appears to 'swim' or 'float' like fish or seaweed in the water. The bold gestural strokes within the forms enhance this floating movement.

Abi Kremer's maturity as an artist is evident for all to see. She continues to enjoy experimenting with her work, developing a range of individual techniques and styles of painting throughout her career. Many benefit from her contribution to the visual arts and we still have more to see as Kremer continues to create work based on life and personal experience.

Jackie Sarafopoulos

Jackie Sarafopoulos is an independent curator who has wide experience of developing exhibitions and art projects. She has had a varied career in arts organisations / cultural institutions and was Exhibitions Officer at the Russell-Cotes Art Gallery and Museum for some years. She has written and contributed to a variety of publications.

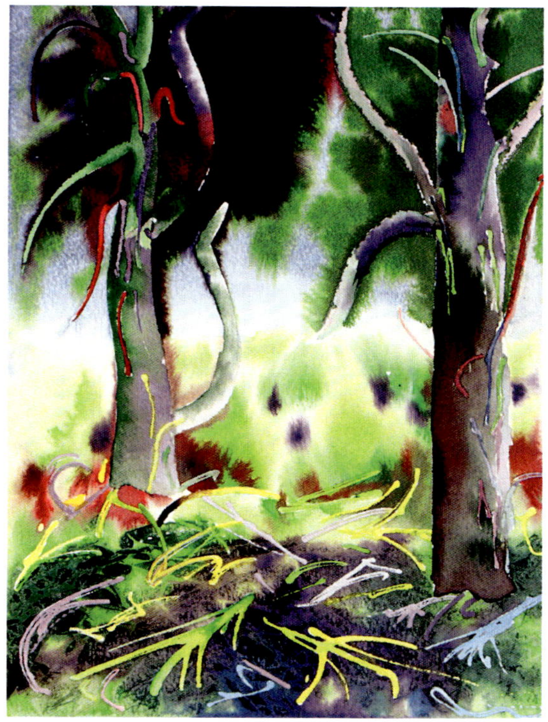

Treescape 3 2008
Watercolour
30cm x 20cm

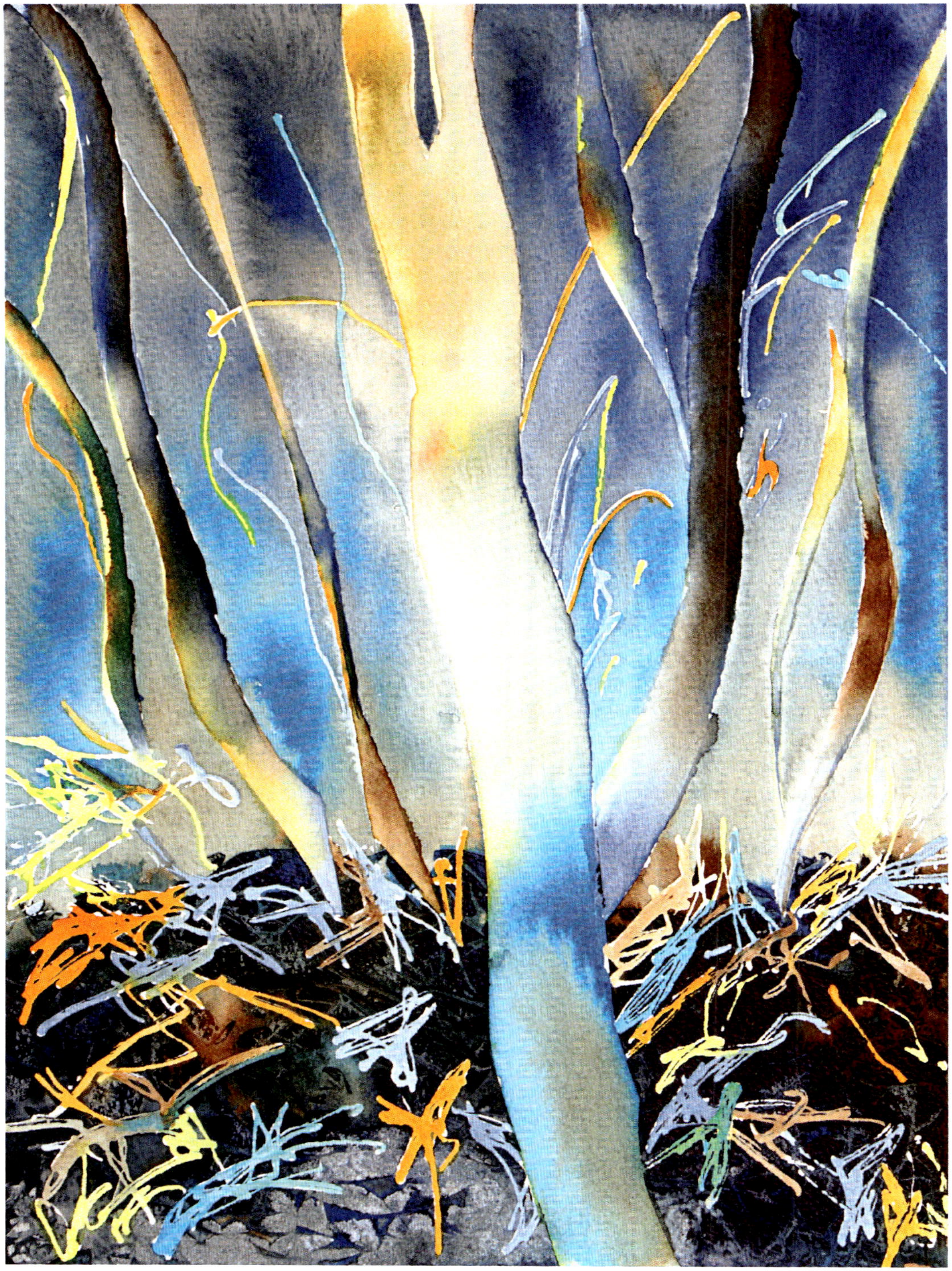

Treescape 2 2008
Watercolour
30cm x 20cm

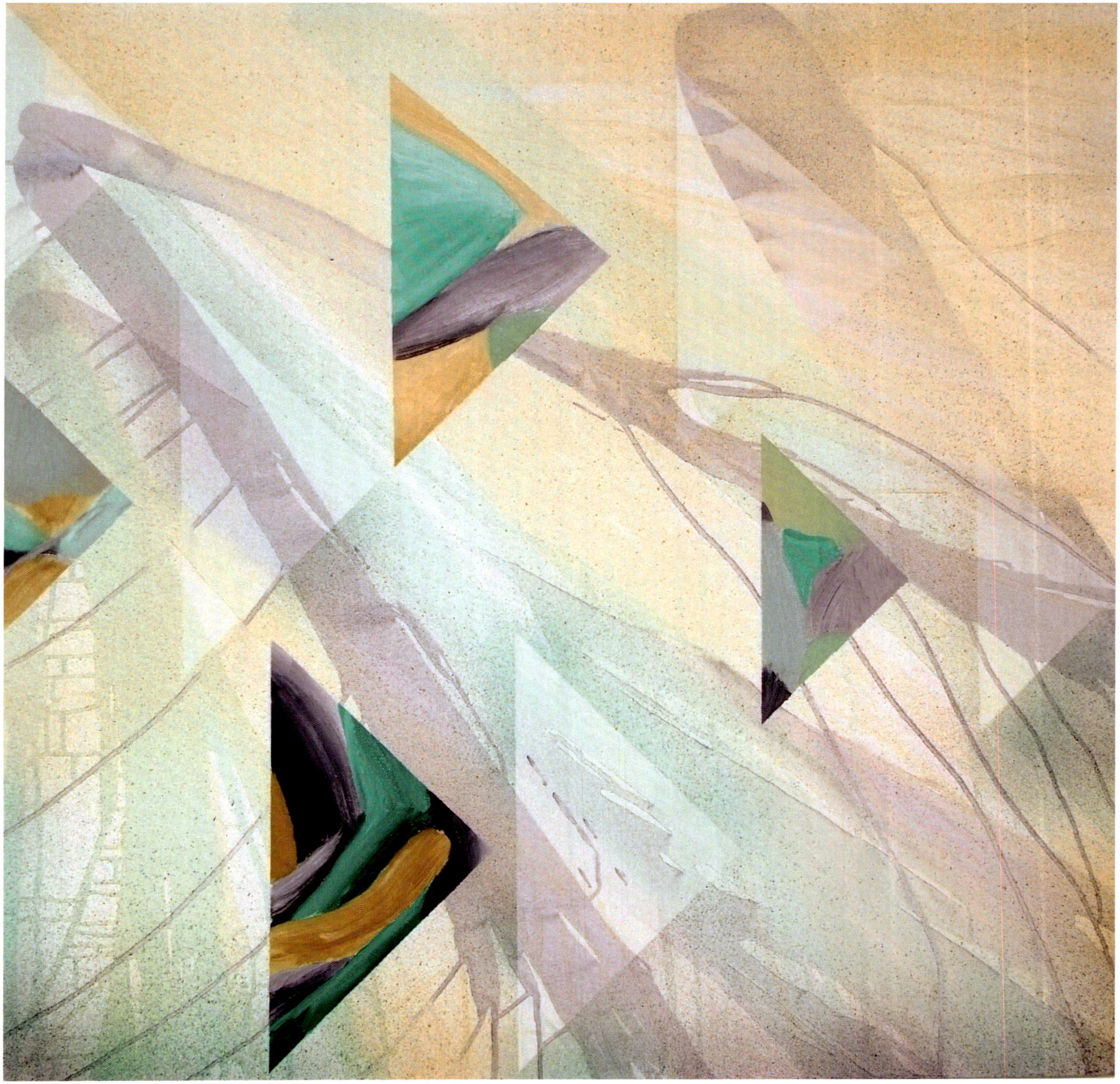

Emerald Movement 2009
Oil on canvas
90cm x 90cm

Abi Kremer

Biography

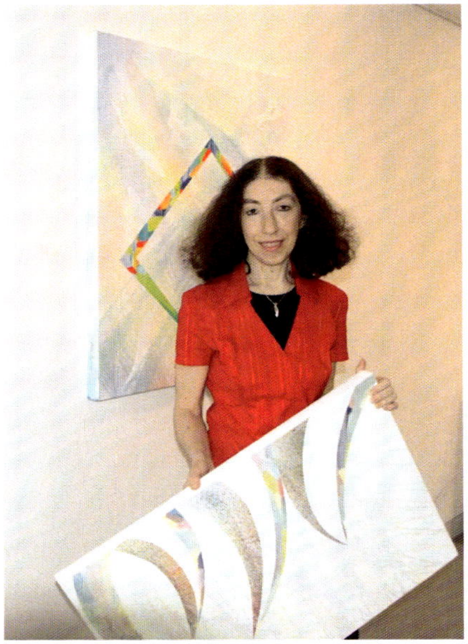

1973 -74	Harrow College of Art
1974-77	Bournemouth College of Art
1992	Fine Art Lecturer Bournemouth and Poole College
1993	Adult Education Art tutor Poole
1994	Adult Education Art tutor Bournemouth
1996	Fine Art Lecturer Southampton University

Abi Kremer

Public Art and Awards

2006	Award: Arts Council England Holton Lee Arts Project
2005	Award: Community Arts Fund Holton Lee Arts Project
2003	Work acquired for RNLI New Building Poole. Dorset
2002	Public Commission Royal Golden Jubilee Glass Plaque New Bournemouth Library
2000	Public Commission Millennium Project: Baby Hand Print Bournemouth Borough Council
2000	Award: Bournemouth Arts Grant Public Commission for Christchurch Hospital
1999	Award: Christchurch Arts Council Public Commission for Somerford Youth Club
1996	Award: Bournemouth Arts Grant Public Commission for Royal Bournemouth Hospital
1993	Award: Bournemouth Arts Grant Odstock Hospital Exhibition
1993	Work acquired for collection of Russell-Cotes Art Gallery and Museum

Garden 2 illustration and a biography are featured in:
"Art in Poole and Dorset" by Peter Davies
Published 1987 (Poole Historical Trust)

Moderntimes@live.co.uk

Abi Kremer

Selected Exhibitions

2009	Abi Kremer: Colour and Inspiration Paintings 1979 - 2009 Kube Poole
2008	Dorset Art Week Light Exhibition Faith House Holton Lee
2007	A Postcard from St .Ives Belgrave Gallery
2006	Works on Canvas Solo exhibition Highcliffe Castle
2005	Works on Paper Solo exhibition Russell-Cotes Art Gallery and Museum
2004	Contemporary Collection Russell-Cotes Art Gallery and Museum
2002	Dorset Art Week Dorset Colourists 3 person exhibition Russell-Cotes Art Gallery and Museum
2001	Salthouse Gallery St. Ives
1995	Solo Exhibition Royal Bournemouth Hospital
1995	Blue Beatrice Royal Art Gallery. Eastleigh
1993	The Land and the Sea Joint exhibition with Martyn Brewster Russell-Cotes Art Gallery and Museum
1990	Solo Exhibition The Gantry. Southampton
1989	My Generation Atkinson Gallery. Southport
1989	Solo Exhibition Old Town Hall Gallery. Havant
1987	Solo Exhibition Seldown Gallery. Poole Arts Centre
1982	Six Artists at the Brewhouse Brewhouse Arts Centre. Taunton
1979	Modern Artists Exhibition Russell-Cotes Art Gallery and Museum
1978	Exhibition in conjunction with Ballet Rambert Poole Arts Centre

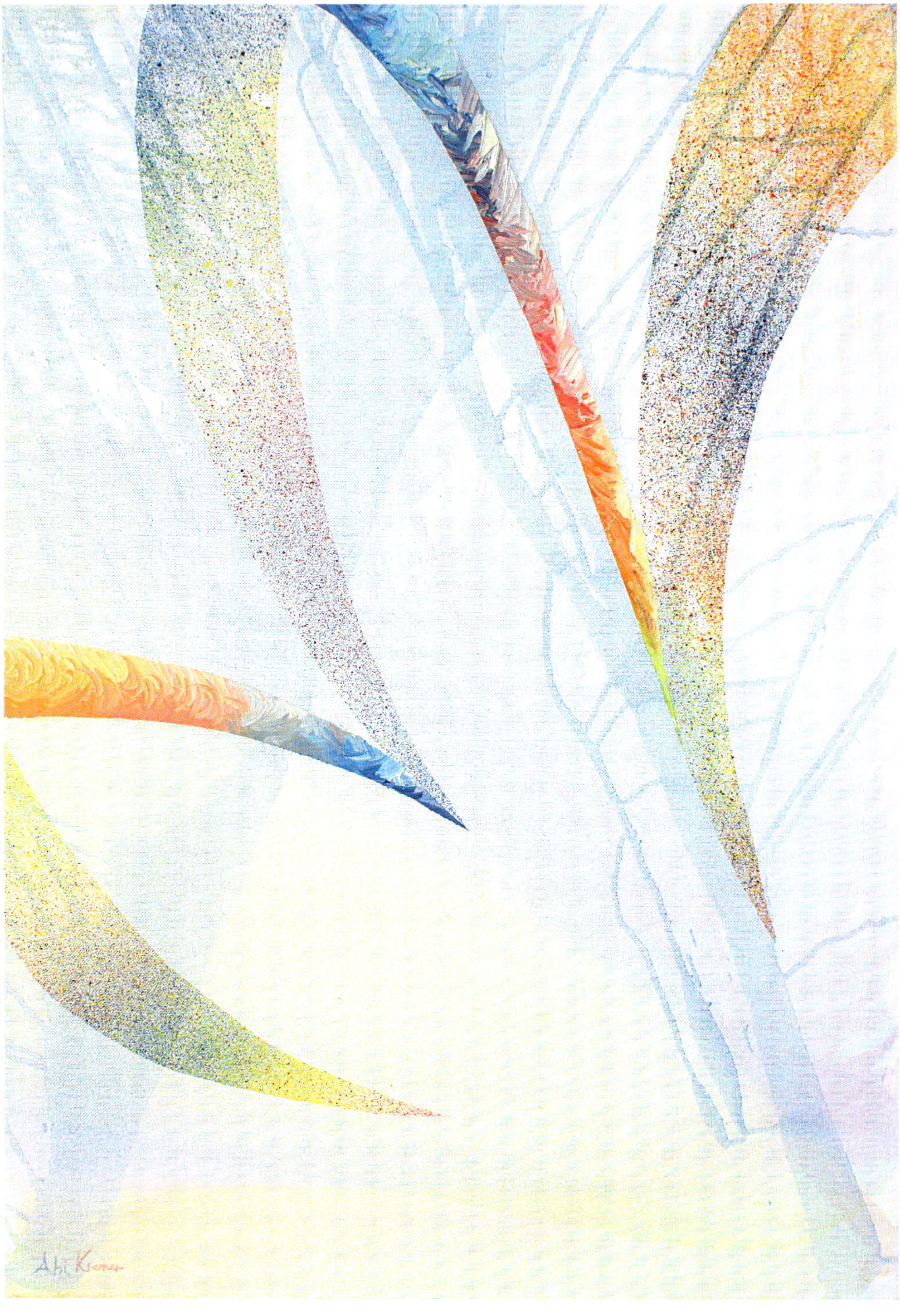

Kami 2007
Oil on canvas
75cm x 50cm

Acknowledgements

Jackie Sarafopoulos for originating the idea of writing this book and her central involvement in its creation. Many thanks are due to the following for their kindness in supporting this publication:

Professor Simon Olding
Peter Davies
Martin Morris
Jonny and Daniel Kremer
Bournemouth and Poole College
Bournemouth and Poole Adult Learning
Southampton City Art Gallery
Arts Council England
Staff, past and present at Holton Lee
Mandy Schaller Photography
Kube
Friends and students of the artist

www.axisweb.org/artist/abikremer